TABLE O

Secret Key #1 - Time is Your Greatest Enemy

Pace Yourself

Wear a watch. At the beginning of the test, check the time (or start a chronometer on your watch to count the minutes), and check the time after every few questions to make sure you are "on schedule."

If you are forced to speed up, do it efficiently. Usually one or more answer choices can be eliminated without too much difficulty. Above all, don't panic. Don't speed up and just begin guessing at random choices. By pacing yourself, and continually monitoring your progress against your watch, you will always know exactly how far ahead or behind you are with your available time. If you find that you are one minute behind on the test, don't skip one question without spending any time on it, just to catch back up. Take 15 fewer seconds on the next four questions, and after four questions you'll have caught back up. Once you catch back up, you can continue working each problem at your normal pace.

Furthermore, don't dwell on the problems that you were rushed on. If a problem was taking up too much time and you made a hurried guess, it must be difficult. The difficult questions are the ones you are most likely to miss anyway, so it isn't a big loss. It is better to end with more time than you need than to run out of time.

Lastly, sometimes it is beneficial to slow down if you are constantly getting ahead of time. You are always more likely to catch a careless mistake by working more slowly than quickly, and among very high-scoring test takers (those who are likely to have lots of time left over), careless errors affect the score more than mastery of material.

Secret Key #2 - Guessing is not Guesswork

You probably know that guessing is a good idea - unlike other standardized tests, there is no penalty for getting a wrong answer. Even if you have no idea about a question, you still have a 20-25% chance of getting it right.

Most test takers do not understand the impact that proper guessing can have on their score. Unless you score extremely high, guessing will significantly contribute to your final score.

Monkeys Take the Test

What most test takers don't realize is that to insure that 20-25% chance, you have to guess randomly. If you put 20 monkeys in a room to take this test, assuming they answered once per question and behaved themselves, on average they would get 20-25% of the questions correct. Put 20 test takers in the room, and the average will be much lower among guessed questions. Why?

1. The test writers intentionally writes deceptive answer choices that "look" right. A test taker has no idea about a question, so picks the "best looking" answer, which is often wrong. The monkey has no idea what looks good and what doesn't, so will consistently be lucky about 20-25% of the time.
2. Test takers will eliminate answer choices from the guessing pool

based on a hunch or intuition. Simple but correct answers often get excluded, leaving a 0% chance of being correct. The monkey has no clue, and often gets lucky with the best choice.

This is why the process of elimination endorsed by most test courses is flawed and detrimental to your performance- test takers don't guess, they make an ignorant stab in the dark that is usually worse than random.

$5 Challenge

Let me introduce one of the most valuable ideas of this course- the $5 challenge:

You only mark your "best guess" if you are willing to bet $5 on it.
You only eliminate choices from guessing if you are willing to bet $5 on it.

Why $5? Five dollars is an amount of money that is small yet not insignificant, and can really add up fast (20 questions could cost you $100). Likewise, each answer choice on one question of the test will have a small impact on your overall score, but it can really add up to a lot of points in the end.

The process of elimination IS valuable. The following shows your chance of guessing it right:

If you eliminate wrong answer choices until only this many remain:	Chance of getting it correct:
1	100%
2	50%
3	33%

However, if you accidentally eliminate the right answer or go on a hunch for an incorrect answer, your chances drop dramatically: to 0%. By guessing among

all the answer choices, you are GUARANTEED to have a shot at the right answer.

That's why the $5 test is so valuable- if you give up the advantage and safety of a pure guess, it had better be worth the risk.

What we still haven't covered is how to be sure that whatever guess you make is truly random. Here's the easiest way:

Always pick the first answer choice among those remaining.

Such a technique means that you have decided, **before you see a single test question**, exactly how you are going to guess- and since the order of choices tells you nothing about which one is correct, this guessing technique is perfectly random.

This section is not meant to scare you away from making educated guesses or eliminating choices- you just need to define when a choice is worth eliminating. The $5 test, along with a pre-defined random guessing strategy, is the best way to make sure you reap all of the benefits of guessing.

Secret Key #3 - Practice Smarter, Not Harder

Many test takers delay the test preparation process because they dread the awful amounts of practice time they think necessary to succeed on the test. We have refined an effective method that will take you only a fraction of the time.

There are a number of "obstacles" in your way to succeed. Among these are answering questions, finishing in time, and mastering test-taking strategies. All must be executed on the day of the test at peak performance, or your score will suffer. The test is a mental marathon that has a large impact on your future.

Just like a marathon runner, it is important to work your way up to the full challenge. So first you just worry about questions, and then time, and finally strategy:

Success Strategy

1. Find a good source for practice tests.
2. If you are willing to make a larger time investment, consider using more than one study guide- often the different approaches of multiple authors will help you "get" difficult concepts.
3. Take a practice test with no time constraints, with all study helps "open book." Take your time with questions and focus on applying strategies.
4. Take a practice test with time constraints, with all guides "open book."
5. Take a final practice test with no open material and time limits.

If you have time to take more practice tests, just repeat step 5. By gradually exposing yourself to the full rigors of the test environment, you will condition your mind to the stress of test day and maximize your success.

Secret Key #4 - Prepare, Don't Procrastinate

Let me state an obvious fact: if you take the test three times, you will get three different scores. This is due to the way you feel on test day, the level of preparedness you have, and, despite the test writers' claims to the contrary, some tests WILL be easier for you than others.

Since your future depends so much on your score, you should maximize your chances of success. In order to maximize the likelihood of success, you've got to prepare in advance. This means taking practice tests and spending time learning the information and test taking strategies you will need to succeed.

Never take the test as a "practice" test, expecting that you can just take it again if you need to. Feel free to take sample tests on your own, but when you go to take the official test, be prepared, be focused, and do your best the first time!

Secret Key #5 - Test Yourself

Everyone knows that time is money. There is no need to spend too much of your time or too little of your time preparing for the test. You should only spend as much of your precious time preparing as is necessary for you to get the score you need.

Once you have taken a practice test under real conditions of time constraints, then you will know if you are ready for the test or not.

If you have scored extremely high the first time that you take the practice test, then there is not much point in spending countless hours studying. You are already there.

Benchmark your abilities by retaking practice tests and seeing how much you have improved. Once you score high enough to guarantee success, then you are ready.

If you have scored well below where you need, then knuckle down and begin studying in earnest. Check your improvement regularly through the use of practice tests under real conditions. Above all, don't worry, panic, or give up. The key is perseverance!

Then, when you go to take the test, remain confident and remember how well you did on the practice tests. If you can score high enough on a practice test, then you can do the same on the real thing.

General Strategies

The most important thing you can do is to ignore your fears and jump into the test immediately- do not be overwhelmed by any strange-sounding terms. You have to jump into the test like jumping into a pool- all at once is the easiest way.

Make Predictions

As you read and understand the question, try to guess what the answer will be. Remember that several of the answer choices are wrong, and once you begin reading them, your mind will immediately become cluttered with answer choices designed to throw you off. Your mind is typically the most focused immediately after you have read the question and digested its contents. If you can, try to predict what the correct answer will be.

You may be surprised at what you can predict.

Quickly scan the choices and see if your prediction is in the listed answer choices. If it is, then you can be quite confident that you have the right answer. It still won't hurt to check the other answer choices, but most of the time, you've got it!

Answer the Question

It may seem obvious to only pick answer choices that answer the question, but the test writers can create some excellent answer choices that are wrong. Don't pick an answer just because it sounds right, or you believe it to be true. It MUST answer the question. Once you've made your selection, always go back and check it against the question and make sure that you didn't misread the question, and the answer choice does answer the question posed.

Benchmark

After you read the first answer choice, decide if you think it sounds correct or not. If it doesn't, move on to the next answer choice. If it does, mentally mark that answer choice. This doesn't mean that you've definitely selected it as your answer choice, it just means that it's the best you've seen thus far. Go ahead and read the next choice. If the next choice is worse than the one you've already selected, keep going to the next answer choice. If the next choice is better than the choice you've already selected, mentally mark the new answer choice as your best guess.

The first answer choice that you select becomes your standard. Every other answer choice must be benchmarked against that standard. That choice is correct until proven otherwise by another answer choice beating it out. Once you've decided that no other answer choice seems as good, do one final check to ensure that your answer choice answers the question posed.

Valid Information

Don't discount any of the information provided in the question. Every piece of information may be necessary to determine the correct answer. None of the information in the question is there to throw you off (while the answer choices will certainly have information to throw you off). If two seemingly unrelated topics are discussed, don't ignore either. You can be confident there is a relationship, or it wouldn't be included in the question, and you are probably going to have to determine what is that relationship to find the answer.

Avoid "Fact Traps"

Don't get distracted by a choice that is factually true. Your search is for the answer that answers the question. Stay focused and don't fall for an answer that is true but incorrect. Always go back to the question and make sure you're choosing an answer that actually answers the question and is not just a true statement. An answer can be factually correct, but it MUST answer the question asked. Additionally, two answers can both be seemingly correct, so be sure to read all of the answer choices, and make sure that you get the one that BEST answers the question.

Milk the Question

Some of the questions may throw you completely off. They might deal with a subject you have not been exposed to, or one that you haven't reviewed in years. While your lack of knowledge about the subject will be a hindrance, the question

itself can give you many clues that will help you find the correct answer. Read the question carefully and look for clues. Watch particularly for adjectives and nouns describing difficult terms or words that you don't recognize. Regardless of if you completely understand a word or not, replacing it with a synonym either provided or one you more familiar with may help you to understand what the questions are asking. Rather than wracking your mind about specific detailed information concerning a difficult term or word, try to use mental substitutes that are easier to understand.

The Trap of Familiarity

Don't just choose a word because you recognize it. On difficult questions, you may not recognize a number of words in the answer choices. The test writers don't put "make-believe" words on the test; so don't think that just because you only recognize all the words in one answer choice means that answer choice must be correct. If you only recognize words in one answer choice, then focus on that one. Is it correct? Try your best to determine if it is correct. If it is, that is great, but if it doesn't, eliminate it. Each word and answer choice you eliminate increases your chances of getting the question correct, even if you then have to guess among the unfamiliar choices.

Eliminate Answers

Eliminate choices as soon as you realize they are wrong. But be careful! Make sure you consider all of the possible answer choices. Just because one appears right, doesn't mean that the next one won't be even better! The test writers will usually put more than one good answer choice for every question, so read all of them. Don't worry if you are stuck between two that seem right. By getting down to just two remaining possible choices, your odds are now 50/50. Rather than wasting too much time, play the odds. You are guessing, but guessing wisely, because you've been able to knock out some of the answer choices that you know are wrong. If you are eliminating choices and realize that the last answer choice you are left with is also obviously wrong, don't panic. Start over and consider each choice again. There may easily be something that you missed the first time and will realize on the second pass.

Tough Questions

If you are stumped on a problem or it appears too hard or too difficult, don't waste time. Move on! Remember though, if you can quickly check for obviously incorrect answer choices, your chances of guessing correctly are greatly improved. Before you completely give up, at least try to knock out a couple of possible answers. Eliminate what you can and then guess at the remaining answer choices before moving on.

Brainstorm

If you get stuck on a difficult question, spend a few seconds quickly brainstorming. Run through the complete list of possible answer choices. Look at each choice and ask yourself, "Could this answer the question satisfactorily?" Go through each answer choice and consider it independently of the other. By systematically going through all possibilities, you may find something that you would otherwise overlook. Remember that when you get stuck, it's important to try to keep moving.

Read Carefully

Understand the problem. Read the question and answer choices carefully. Don't miss the question because you misread the terms. You have plenty of time to read each question thoroughly and make sure you understand what is being asked. Yet a happy medium must be attained, so don't waste too much time. You must read carefully, but efficiently.

Face Value

When in doubt, use common sense. Always accept the situation in the problem at face value. Don't read too much into it. These problems will not require you to make huge leaps of logic. The test writers aren't trying to throw you off with a cheap trick. If you have to go beyond creativity and make a leap of logic in order to have an answer choice answer the question, then you should look at the other answer choices. Don't overcomplicate the problem by creating theoretical relationships or explanations that will warp time or space. These are normal problems rooted in reality. It's just that the applicable relationship or explanation may not be readily apparent and you have to figure things out. Use your common sense to interpret anything that isn't clear.

Prefixes

If you're having trouble with a word in the question or answer choices, try dissecting it. Take advantage of every clue that the word might include. Prefixes and suffixes can be a huge help. Usually they allow you to determine a basic meaning. Pre- means before, post- means after, pro - is positive, de- is negative. From these prefixes and suffixes, you can get an idea of the general meaning of the word and try to put it into context. Beware though of any traps. Just because con is the opposite of pro, doesn't necessarily mean congress is the opposite of progress!

Hedge Phrases

Watch out for critical "hedge" phrases, such as likely, may, can, will often, sometimes, often, almost, mostly, usually, generally, rarely, sometimes. Question writers insert these hedge phrases to cover every possibility. Often an answer choice will be wrong simply because it leaves no room for exception. Avoid answer choices that have definitive words like "exactly," and "always".

Switchback Words

Stay alert for "switchbacks". These are the words and phrases frequently used to alert you to shifts in thought. The most common switchback word is "but". Others include although, however, nevertheless, on the other hand, even though, while, in spite of, despite, regardless of.

New Information

Correct answer choices will rarely have completely new information included. Answer choices typically are straightforward reflections of the material asked about and will directly relate to the question. If a new piece of information is included in an answer choice that doesn't even seem to relate to the topic being asked about, then that answer choice is likely incorrect. All of the information needed to answer the question is usually provided for you, and so you should not have to make guesses that are unsupported or choose answer choices that require unknown information that cannot be reasoned on its own.

Time Management

On technical questions, don't get lost on the technical terms. Don't spend too much time on any one question. If you don't know what a term means, then since you don't have a dictionary, odds are you aren't going to get much further. You should immediately recognize terms as whether or not you know them. If you don't, work with the other clues that you have, the other answer choices and terms provided, but don't waste too much time trying to figure out a difficult term.

Contextual Clues

Look for contextual clues. An answer can be right but not correct. The contextual clues will help you find the answer that is most right and is correct. Understand the context in which a phrase or statement is made. This will help you make important distinctions.

Don't Panic

Panicking will not answer any questions for you. Therefore, it isn't helpful. When you first see the question, if your mind goes blank, take a deep breath. Force yourself to mechanically go through the steps of solving the problem and using the strategies you've learned.

Pace Yourself

Don't get clock fever. It's easy to be overwhelmed when you're looking at a page full of questions, your mind is full of random thoughts and feeling confused, and the clock is ticking down faster than you would like. Calm down and maintain the pace that you have set for yourself. As long as you are on track by monitoring your pace, you are guaranteed to have enough time for yourself. When you get to the last few minutes of the test, it may seem like you won't have enough time left, but if you only have as many questions as you should have left at that point, then you're right on track!

Answer Selection

The best way to pick an answer choice is to eliminate all of those that are wrong, until only one is left and confirm that is the correct answer. Sometimes though, an answer choice may immediately look right. Be careful! Take a second to make sure that the other choices are not equally obvious. Don't make a hasty mistake. There are only two times that you should stop before checking other answers. First is when you are positive that the answer choice you have selected is correct. Second is when time is almost out and you have to make a quick guess!

Check Your Work

Since you will probably not know every term listed and the answer to every question, it is important that you get credit for the ones that you do know. Don't miss any questions through careless mistakes. If at all possible, try to take a second to look back over your answer selection and make sure you've selected the correct answer choice and haven't made a costly careless mistake (such as marking an answer choice that you didn't mean to mark). This quick double check should more than pay for itself in caught mistakes for the time it costs.

Beware of Directly Quoted

Answers

Sometimes an answer choice will repeat word for word a portion of the question or reference section. However, beware of such exact duplication – it may be a trap! More than likely, the correct choice will paraphrase or summarize a point, rather than being exactly the same wording.

Slang

Scientific sounding answers are better than slang ones. An answer choice that begins "To compare the outcomes..." is much more likely to be correct than one that begins "Because some people insisted..."

Extreme Statements

Avoid wild answers that throw out highly controversial ideas that are proclaimed as established fact. An answer choice that states the "process should used in certain situations, if..." is much more likely to be correct than one that states the "process should be discontinued completely." The first is a calm rational statement and doesn't even make a definitive, uncompromising stance, using a hedge word "if" to provide wiggle room, whereas the second choice is a radical idea and far more extreme.

Answer Choice Families

When you have two or more answer choices that are direct opposites or parallels, one of them is usually the correct answer. For instance, if one answer choice states "x increases" and another answer choice states "x decreases" or "y increases," then those two or three answer choices are very similar in construction and fall into the same family of answer choices. A family of answer choices is when two or three answer choices are very similar in construction, and yet often have a directly opposite meaning. Usually the correct answer choice will be in that family of answer choices. The "odd man out" or answer choice that doesn't seem to fit the parallel construction of the other answer choices is more likely to be incorrect.

Top 20 Test Taking Tips

1. Carefully follow all the test registration procedures
2. Know the test directions, duration, topics, question types, how many questions
3. Setup a flexible study schedule at least 3-4 weeks before test day
4. Study during the time of day you are most alert, relaxed, and stress free
5. Maximize your learning style; visual learner use visual study aids, auditory learner use auditory study aids
6. Focus on your weakest knowledge base
7. Find a study partner to review with and help clarify questions
8. Practice, practice, practice
9. Get a good night's sleep; don't try to cram the night before the test
10. Eat a well balanced meal
11. Know the exact physical location of the testing site; drive the route to the site prior to test day
12. Bring a set of ear plugs; the testing center could be noisy
13. Wear comfortable, loose fitting, layered clothing to the testing center; prepare for it to be either cold or hot during the test
14. Bring at least 2 current forms of ID to the testing center
15. Arrive to the test early; be prepared to wait and be patient
16. Eliminate the obviously wrong answer choices, then guess the first remaining choice
17. Pace yourself; don't rush, but keep working and move on if you get stuck
18. Maintain a positive attitude even if the test is going poorly
19. Keep your first answer unless you are positive it is wrong
20. Check your work, don't make a careless mistake

Integration of Foundations

Educational goals

The Association for Career and Technical Education has identified nine goals commonly associated with education. These nine goals are to:

- Improve the overall quality of life for individuals and families.
- Help individuals and families become responsible members of society.
- Encourage healthy eating habits, nutrition, and lifestyles.
- Improve how individuals and families manage their resources.
- Help individuals and families balance their personal, family, and work roles.
- Teach individuals better problem-solving techniques.
- Encourage personal and career development.
- Teach individuals to successfully function as both consumers and providers.
- Recognize human worth and take responsibility for ones own actions.

Quality of life

The first of the nine goals established for education is to improve the overall quality of life for individuals and families, which is also the primary mission that all of the goals aid in accomplishing. Education teaches people about how individuals, families, and the rest of society interact with each other and methods for improving those interactions. These methods include problem-solving techniques, common scams and problems to avoid, methods to stay healthy both physically and psychologically, and a variety of other information regarding how the individual, family, and the rest of society functions. Ultimately, the primary goal of education is to improve the quality of life by educating individuals and families in the best manner to function on a day to day basis. However, this goal is only really accomplished when the other eight goals of education are completed.

Sexual stereotypes

Eliminating sexual stereotypes is a major concern of education as it is important that an individual is able to disregard sexual stereotypes and recognize that an individual's gender does not necessarily affect the role a particular individual plays. In the early to mid 1900's, women were commonly seen as caretakers of the home and men as providers for the family. However, these roles have changed drastically over the past fifty to sixty years and it is important that individuals realize that it may not be realistically possible for women and men to play these roles any longer. For an individual or family to function appropriately, there are certain necessities that must be acquired and as the cost of living increases, it becomes more and more difficult for a single individual to provide for the entire family. As a result, both men and women need to share the caretaker and provider roles to satisfy the physiological, financial, and psychological needs of the family.

Balancing roles

It is important that an individual is able to balance his or her work and home roles because it is becoming more and more common for individuals to have to act as both caregiver and provider for the family. The ever more common presence of dual roles in society can be extremely difficult for an individual to balance as there may be instances where work-related responsibilities and family-related responsibilities conflict with one another. education attempts to teach individuals how to avoid and how to handle these conflicts through the use of successful life management tactics such as time and resources management, problem-solving and decision-making techniques, effective communication techniques, etc. education also attempts to give individuals a basic understanding of what responsibilities and qualities are necessary for the successful completion of each role so that individuals can set better priorities and find better ways to plan their lives.

Skill types

There are three types of skills and indications about whether those skills are being used effectively:

- An individual's level of affective skill refers to how effectively an individual can recognize, understand, and handle emotions, relationships, and other social interaction. Affective skills allow an individual to feel a certain emotion as a result of a certain situation or stimuli and then respond based on that emotion. Some of the factors that can be used to measure how well-developed an individual's affective skills are include determining how well the individual receives emotional stimuli and how well the individual responds to those stimuli. It is also important to determine how easy it is for the individual to acknowledge the worth of a particular situation, relationship, or individual and whether or not the individual has an organized and well-conceived value system. An individual's ability to receive and respond to emotional stimuli can be measured by how aware the individual is of a particular stimulus, how willing the individual is to acknowledge that particular stimulus, and how focused the individual is on that stimulus. An individual's ability to assign value to a situation and uphold a value system can be measured by how motivated the individual is, how the individual behaves, and how consistent is that individual's behavior. For example, a student that always comes to class and clearly always pays attention may have well-developed affective skills.

- An individual's level of cognitive skill refers to an individual's ability to gather and understand information. Cognitive skills allow an individual to comprehend and apply knowledge that they have already gathered in other situations. Some of the factors that can be used to measure how well-developed an individual's cognitive skills are include determining the individual's ability to retain knowledge, comprehend knowledge, apply knowledge, and evaluate knowledge. An individual's ability to retain knowledge can be measured by testing the individual's ability to remember certain facts and information through exams or simply asking questions. An individual's ability to comprehend knowledge can be measured by an individual demonstrating a concept in a different form, explaining a concept in more detail or simplifying a concept, or

- 15 -

predicting a result based on a particular concept. An individual breaking a concept down into individual parts and demonstrating how those parts make up the whole can also show comprehension of a particular concept. An individual's ability to apply knowledge can be measured by an individual demonstrating that they can use a particular concept for a real-life purpose. Finally, an individual's ability to evaluate a particular piece of knowledge can be indicated by the individual showing the value of that knowledge.

- An individual's level of psychomotor skill refers to an individual's ability to control his or her physical movements as well as his or her coordination. In other words, psychomotor skills are the ability that an individual has to control his or her simple and complex motor functions. Some of the factors that can be used to measure how well-developed an individual's psychomotor skills are include how well an individual performs physical skills and acts, how precisely can the individual perform those skills or activities, and how natural do those activities seem to be for the individual. An individual's ability to use physical skills can be measured simply by how much difficulty the individual has in accomplishing a particular complex physical activity such as climbing a rope or assembling a model. How precisely the individual can perform those skills or activities can be measured by determining the quality of the end result of the individual's physical activity and

how long it took the individual to reach that result. For example, if the individual has constructed a model plane, does the model look like a plane, are its wings and other parts attached correctly, how long it took to assemble, etc. Finally, an activity is natural for an individual if the individual can perform it without thinking.

Skills used everyday

It is extremely important for an individual to be able to use a combination of his or her affective, cognitive, and psychomotor skills together on a day-to-day basis as each type of skill is essential to the overall functioning of a healthy individual. An individual that has mastered his or her psychomotor skills may be in excellent physical health, but the individual's overall health as well as the health of the individual's family will suffer if the individual is unable to make effective relationships and understand basic and complex concepts. The situation is the same for an individual that can only make effective relationships or who can only understand complex concepts as it will be significantly more difficult for the individual to perform everyday functions if the individual has poor control over his or her psychomotor skills. For an individual to maintain the physical and mental health of the individual and his or her family, the individual has to be able to use a combination of different skills.

Professional organizations

Professional organizations such as the American Association of , also known as the AAFCS, play an important role in influencing the education of individuals in the methodology and knowledge associated with . Many of these local and national professional organizations offer seminars, courses, and publications directly to individuals and families to help them learn how to improve essential career and management skills, how to be smart consumers, give them information about proper nutrition, and information about a wide range of other topics. These professional organizations also usually offer publications, advice, and curriculum guides to teachers, professors, and other education professionals that help these professionals teach and stay informed regarding important changes to the curriculum that occur as societal norms change. These organizations also have a profound effect on family and consumer science education by influencing public policy and gathering support for programs that help educate and protect individuals and families from unsafe habits, business practices, products, and lifestyles.

Family and consumer education

Family and consumer education is a teaching discipline that attempts to teach and improve a variety of skills that are essential for the day-to-day functioning of an individual and his or her family. Family and consumer education includes educating individuals in specific topics such as family interaction, human development, nutrition, consumer economics, types of housing and housing design, textiles, parenting, appropriate cooking and handling of foods, and a variety of other topics necessary for an individual to continue functioning successfully. Family and consumer education covers information about both the physical needs of the individual and the psychological needs of the individual and puts a large emphasis on the necessity of appropriate social interaction between the individual and the rest of society. Individuals in the family and consumer education field are teachers, professors, and other education professionals as the purpose of the

discipline is to educate individuals in techniques that they can use in their daily lives to improve their overall well being.

There are several concepts that are at the core of family and consumer education, but one of the most important concepts is that families are the basic unit of society. Humans do not function well in solitary environments and therefore they usually live together in groups and the basic groups that make up society are families. Another important concept of family and consumer education is that individuals need to be life-long learners in order to develop and function appropriately. This means that each individual needs to be taught the skills necessary to gather information in the future. Finally, family and consumer education believes that individuals and families need to have an understanding of the advantages of different methods and diverse ways of thinking in order to solve any given problem.

There are a large number of methods that an educator can use to demonstrate concepts related to , but the best methods always involve promoting the students' active participation. Some examples of demonstrations that promote active participation are allowing students to use a sewing machine, having students test the qualities of various textiles to see how soft, lustrous, resilient, absorbent, etc. each material is, and having students prepare a meal. Some other examples of valid demonstration methods include comparing advertisements to find the best offer and examine common marketing tactics, allowing students to visit or work-in a local day-care center, or getting students involved in local community service activities. Many of these activities not only act as an effective way of teaching students about the important concepts of , but also act as a means of testing the student's ability to apply the techniques and information that they have learned.

Occupational education

Occupational education is a teaching discipline that is similar to the standard discipline of family and consumer education, but focuses less on the skills for day-to-day living and more on how those skills can be used in the workplace. Occupational education covers information regarding skills that can commonly be applied in fields such as health services, food service, child care, hospitality, fashion design, interior design, and many other similar fields. Occupational places more emphasis on family and consumer skills that can be directly related to use in a career, such as management techniques and ethical businesses practices, than the standard family and consumer education discipline. This educational discipline ultimately takes the skills that an individual has learned from the standard discipline and shows how those skills can be applied to a career.

Community advisory committees

Community advisory committees can be extremely useful to an education professional that is attempting to determine what areas of the family and consumer science discipline a class should focus on because they offer insight into the concerns and demographics of the students. Each community has its own separate problems, concerns, and level of diversity and it is important that a family and consumer science teacher can recognize and focus on areas of concern that the students may require more improvement in than students from other communities. For example, a community that is having problems with wide spread teenage drug abuse and teenage suicide may want the community's family and

consumer science teachers to focus more on avoiding substance abuse and methods of handling depression. The overall goal of a educator is to improve the overall quality of life for the students and their families and the educator cannot do that if he or she does not know what problems need to be addressed.

Some of the functions that community advisory committees perform, other than offering advice to education professionals, include assessing the performance of family and consumer science programs, assessing the performance of students with special needs, and providing equipment, technology, and resources for family and consumer science programs. These resources may include raw materials, textile samples, charts and diagrams, library books, access to computers and design software, etc. Community advisory committees also attempt to help students improve their chances of finding better jobs and careers and act as a sort of public relations department for local family and consumer science programs. Ultimately, the primary purpose of a community advisory committee is to ensure that a program has all of the resources and training necessary to achieve the program's goals and to make sure that the program is moving towards achieving those goals.

Laboratory settings

A laboratory setting can be important for an educator teaching as it offers students an opportunity to gain hands-on experience regarding a variety of skills and techniques. Many of the important areas of the discipline center around using a combination of various skills to achieve a certain end result and sometimes the best way to teach the appropriate manner of integrating these skills is through experience. A laboratory setting offers individuals a place to demonstrate and improve their skills related to the family and consumer science field where an educator can answer questions and correct mistakes. Some examples of useful laboratory settings for the field include kitchens or food science laboratories, day care centers, testing laboratories for textiles or consumer products, and many other similar settings.

Evaluating understanding

Usually, the best method that an educator can use to determine whether or not a student understands a particular concept is to see whether or not the student can actively apply the information that he or she has learned to everyday tasks. These tasks can include activities such as cooking, sewing, time management, etc. It is also possible for an educator to test a student's level of comprehension by administering written tests, assigning projects and research papers, having students design charts and diagrams, evaluating case studies and scenarios, having students keep a journal of their activities and eating habits, and many other similar methods. Which evaluation method an educator should use depends primarily on the material that the program is covering as it may be difficult for an individual to actively demonstrate their understanding of certain concepts if a laboratory setting is not available.

FCCLA

The FCCLA, which stands for the Family, Career, and Community Leaders of America, is a youth organization for students in family and consumer science education. The FCCLA offers a variety of publications and programs designed to educate people about parenting, relationships, substance abuse, teen pregnancy, teen violence, and a variety of other concerns. The primary purpose of these programs is not only to educate, but also to bring public attention to the problems that young people face and in turn gather support for programs and laws that help protect young people and their families. The FCCLA also attempts to help show students how they can improve their family and consumer science skills and apply those skills to finding careers later in life.

The FCCLA and other similar youth organizations play an important role in providing education and influencing national policy related to protecting families and consumers. However, these organizations are also important because they help make other family and consumer science programs more successful. The primary goal of any program is to improve the overall quality of life for the individual and family and the best way to do that is to get people learning about and involved in as early as possible. The students that educators are teaching now will eventually go out and start future families so it is essential that these students can learn the skills that will allow them and their families to live better lives now. The FCCLA and other similar youth organizations play an important role in not only educating people about family and consumer science concepts, but also in allowing students additional opportunities to improve and actively apply their skills.

Consumer science careers

Some of the specific careers that individuals might be able to use their family and consumer science skills in include food management, financial management, human resources, public relations, tailoring, dress-making, etc. Regardless of which career an individual chooses there is almost always some combination of skills that an individual can use both in his or her day-to-day living and in his or her career. An individual in food management can use knowledge about nutritional needs, the proper handling of food, and the temperatures and the amount of time necessary to prepare various foods. Financial advisors can use information regarding how to assess resources, determine the best way to cut costs, and determine how much an individual needs to save before retirement. Human resource and public relations managers can use their social skills and their knowledge of time management, resource management, and of human development and psychology to more effectively carry out their responsibilities. Finally, tailors and dressmakers can use their knowledge of various textiles and textile design to construct better garments.

An educator that is attempting to teach his or her students how to find the appropriate career and the skills that might be necessary for that career may want to begin by offering some examples of different careers. Some of these examples may be directly related to family and consumer science careers, but is also important that the educator identifies some careers that may not be directly related. It is important for the class to examine a diverse sampling of different careers because family and consumer science skills can be applied to virtually any setting and it is essential for an educator to teach his or her students methods of determining how various techniques can be applied. For example, a construction worker might not need to know about food, textiles, or housing design, but he or she still needs to know various problem-solving techniques. It can also be extremely useful if students can get some hands-on experience applying family and consumer science concepts to the tasks associated with various careers.

New legislation

When a new act of legislation is passed, it can often have a profound impact on the type of material that needs to be covered by education. A large part of improving the quality of life for individuals and families is warning individuals about the dangers and unethical practices that exist in the world around them. It is, however, also important that individuals understand the legal protections and rights granted to them by the various acts put into place by each state and the federal government. Since laws are constantly changing and the tactics that unscrupulous individuals and businesses use are changing as well, family and consumer science educators need to be able to adapt quickly and add information regarding new legislation to their curriculum.

Assessing student needs

The first step that an educator should take when determining the best way to meet the special needs of a student should be to determine exactly what the needs of the student are. If the student is performing poorly, the educator needs to determine whether it is because the student does not understand the material or because the student is unmotivated by the material. Each student is unique in his or her ability to learn and comprehend the material and therefore it is important for an educator to determine the cause of the student's poor performance. Once the cause has been identified, the teacher can determine how much assistance is needed. If the student's needs can be met through techniques such as one-on-one attention or assigning special projects, this is usually the best course of action. However, if the student has needs that require solutions beyond simple changes in curriculum, such as potential psychological or physiological disorders, the educator may have to discuss other options with the child's parents.

Assessment validity

The type of technique an educator should use to ensure the validity of an assessment depends on the type of assessment that is being performed. To ensure the validity of a written exam, an educator should consider using an outline of the material that has been covered by the class to design the questions that are included on the test. This allows the educator to make sure that the exam is a valid assessment of how much information the students have learned and understood rather than assessing students on material that may not truly indicate what students have learned in class. An educator that wishes to ensure the validity of a laboratory demonstration being used as an assessment should use a quality checklist to check the laboratory equipment before the demonstration and make sure to observe the students as they work. This allows the educator, to ensure that the laboratory equipment is functioning properly and that the laboratory environment remains uncontaminated by outside influences that may cause a student to fail.

Family Studies and Human Services

Family versus individual

A family is commonly considered a group of people that is related by birth, adoption, or marriage who reside together usually for the purpose of raising children. However, a family can refer to any group of individuals that live together in the same household even if they are not related by blood or legal ties. This means that an unmarried couple who is living together or even a pair of roommates may be considered a family.

A single individual, however, is the opposite of a family as it is a person who lives alone and therefore does not have to regularly interact with relatives or other individuals within the household.

Family structure

The four major types of family structures are nuclear, extended, single-parent, and blended and each of these structures are based on the idea that a family is a group of people who aid in the raising of the next generation.

- A nuclear family is the traditional concept of a family where there is a mother, father, and their children living in the same household.
- An extended family is an expansion of the nuclear family that includes the mother, father, and their children, as well as aunts, uncles, cousins, and grandparents.
- A single-parent structure is simply a family where one parent is the only one in the home caring for the children.

- A blended family, also known as a stepfamily, is when a parent marries or remarries when they already have their own children and there is a parent, stepparent, and one or more children living in the household.

Recent changes

The typical structure of families in the United States has changed drastically in recent years as the norm moves away from the traditional nuclear family towards the ever more common structure of the blended family. As more and more individuals divorce and remarry, blended families become much more common because children are being taken care of by both biological and stepparents more frequently. This increase in the number of blended families, which were virtually unheard of fifty to sixty years ago, has also led the structure of the blended family to be extended into two sub-structures, simple and complex, based on whether both parents have children or not. In a simple stepfamily only one of the individuals marrying has children, but the other does not and in a complex stepfamily both parents marrying have their own children before marriage.

Family stages

There are commonly 9 stages that a family can go through from beginning to end:

- The first stage, which is the single or bachelor stage, is where the individual is yet to be married and the family is not really a family, but rather a single individual.
- The second stage is the newly married couple stage where two individuals have just married, but do not have children yet.
- The third stage is the beginning of the three full nest stages where

- 22 -

the family has children and is attempting to raise them. Full nest stage I is where the youngest child is under 6.

- The fourth stage, full nest stage II, is where the youngest child is 6 or over,
- The fifth stage, full nest stage III, is the stage where an older married couple has dependent children.
- The empty nest I stage is where the head of the household in an older married couple is still in the labor force, but the couple has no children living with them.
- The empty nest II stage is the same as the empty nest I stage except that the head of the household has retired.
- The solitary survivor in labor force stage is when one of the couple has passed away and the survivor must continue to work to support him or herself.
- The final stage, the retired solitary survivor stage, is the same as the solitary survivor in labor force stage, except that the survivor has retired and there are no longer any individuals living in the household still in the labor force.

Purpose of family

The primary purpose of a family is to aid in the survival of the family and nurture the children of the family. Families allow individuals to survive more easily by dividing up the work and tasks necessary to survive by sharing those tasks, such as working and taking care of the home, with the rest of the family. Families also provide emotional support to the members of the family during times of high stress. The family aids in the nurturing of children by offering social and emotional interaction, protecting the children from potential danger, and educating the children in social norms

and customs. The family also provides the basic necessities required, such as food, clothing, shelter, and play, for the basic physical development of the children in the household.

One of the most important functions a family provides is developing and educating the members of the family. Parents and grandparents pass their heritage and teachings of social norms and acceptable behavior to the children of the family through their customs, traditions, and ultimately their actions. Children learn about their heritage through the traditions of the family and also often learn lessons about the manner in which they are expected to behave by using the behavior of their parents and the rest of the household as a model for how the child should behave. Children also learn about the manner in which the world around them functions through the interactions of the members of the family with the world outside of the household. This allows the child to understand more complex types of social interaction such as what goods the family needs, where the family must go to fulfill those needs, and what is needed to acquire those necessities, such as how much money is required to purchase an item.

The following terms with regard to their importance in the development and education of family members:

- Behavioral modeling, when relating to how a child develops within a family structure, is the manner in which a child models their own behavior after the behavior of their parents and other people that interact with them. A child learns what behavior is socially acceptable by mimicking the behavior of the people around them.
- Consumer education is the process of teaching a person to

understand the manner in which the marketplace works specifically in regards to the goods and services available, the suppliers of those goods and services, and the things to look for and look out for when searching for goods and services. These concepts are very important for a family member to learn how to protect themselves and survive in a consumer society.

- Heritage is simply anything that is inherited from one's ancestors such as traditions, customs, or even physical characteristics. The family acts as a medium to convey the traditions, customs, and social norms of the previous generation to the children that follow.

Healthy family roles

There are five major roles that are essential to the functioning of a family, which are providing necessities, development and education, emotional support, management of the family, and satisfying the needs of the married couple. Individuals within the family need to provide necessities by creating income so the family can be supplied with food, clothing, and shelter. Family members need to teach not only customs, but also skills that will help the members of the family successfully advance through school and eventually into a career. Families need to provide emotional support for other family members during times of high stress and the family needs someone to take a leadership role and handle issues such as managing finances and maintaining the roles essential to the family's survival. The married couple also has their own needs, such as basic necessities, sexual needs, and basic emotional needs that need to be met for the family to continue functioning normally.

The following terms are important to keep in mind regarding family roles:

- A role is a series of social rights, behaviors, and obligations that are assigned to a particular individual. For example, a mother's role might be that of a provider as she is out in the workforce attempting to provide income for the family.
- Role confusion is when an individual is uncertain of what role or roles they should play in a particular situation. For example, a nurse might run into a patient whom she took care of previously while out grocery shopping and be unsure of whether to act in a formal, nurse to patient manner or in an informal, friendly manner.
- Role strain is when an individual is placed in a situation that carrying out the duties of a certain role will prevent the individual from fulfilling their obligations to another role. For example, a working mother might be both caregiver and provider and if her child becomes ill she cannot carry out both roles as she is forced to choose between working and caring for the sick child.

Married couples

The married couple, or in some cases simply the couple living together, make up the center of the family and therefore have a profound effect on the relationships and well-being of the family as a whole. If the marital couple is having difficulty in their relationship and the stress of those difficulties becomes apparent, the rest of the family will most likely exhibit signs of the same stress. For example, if the marital couple is consistently seen fighting, or even if they just become withdrawn after a fight has taken place, other members of the family may react to the stress of the married couple and become more withdrawn, upset, or even hostile. On the other hand, marital couples that are not experiencing marital difficulties and seem warm and affectionate will foster the same feelings of warmth and affection in the rest of the family.

Marriage

Marriage is a union, usually between two individuals, that is often held as a legally binding contract for the members of the union stating their intention to live together and aid each other in maintaining a family for the rest of their lives. Even though couples who simply live together in the same household can constitute a family under the commonly used definition, the institution of marriage offers a level of stability to the family structure that is not present when an unmarried couple makes up the center of the family. This added stability is primarily a result of the societal, religious, and governmental recognition of the institution of marriage that creates an expectation that the marriage and ultimately the family will remain intact. Although many married couples eventually separate and divorce, it is more difficult for any member of the marital couple to leave the family than it would be for a member of a couple that had no legal or societal obligation to remain together.

Divorce

Divorce is the termination of the union created by marriage before the death of any member of the union and it has a significant impact upon the stability of the family as a whole as well as affecting the relationships and well-being of the individual members of the family. Often when the marital couple decides to divorce, there has already been significant stress placed upon the entire family from the difficulties the marital couple has been experiencing. However, especially when children are involved, divorce can often lead to a great deal more stress being placed on the family and individuals within and outside the marital couple may become more withdrawn or hostile as the structure of the family changes. Divorce also allows both members of the marital couple to later remarry, as their legal obligation no longer exists, which can alter the family structure further by adding stepparents to the family.

Studies indicate that the age that a couple marries may have a significant impact on whether they remain married for an extended period. Individuals who marry before either member of the couple is 18 will often separate within a few years of their marriage. Individuals who are in the 18-25 range will separate less frequently than those who marry before 18, but are still at a very high risk for their marriage ending in divorce rather than death. Individuals who marry after they are both over 25 have a significantly lower risk of divorce than those who would marry at younger ages. Ultimately, statistics show that the risk of divorce seems to decrease as the age of each member of the couple at the time of the marriage increases.

There are many factors that may influence the risk of a marriage ending in divorce including income, education, religion, pregnancy before marriage, and whether the parents of the married couple are divorced. Couples who make over $50,000 a year are at a much lower risk of seeking a divorce than couples who make less than that amount. Couples that consist of well-educated individuals, who have graduated from high school and have at least some college background, also have a much lower risk of seeking a divorce than less educated individuals. Couples with no religious background or drastically different religious backgrounds have a much higher risk of divorce than couples that have religious backgrounds that do not conflict. Couples that have a baby prior to being married also have a higher risk of divorce than couples who have children after they are married. Individuals with parents who are divorced also have a higher risk of divorce than individuals from families that are intact.

Social and economic factors

Many social and economic factors can influence the overall functioning of a family. In fact, researchers use an index called the socioeconomic status or SES, to measure the ability of the family to function in a healthy fashion. The SES uses the educational background of the members of the family, the family's total income, and the skill, both actual and perceived, required by the occupations of the individuals who act as providers for the family to measure the family's ability to function. Individuals who are well educated tend to marry later in life, receive jobs with higher incomes, and have careers with a higher social status, which all add stability to the marriage and stability to the overall functioning of the family. Families that have a large amount of income are also less concerned with obtaining basic necessities, as the family consistently has the means to obtain them, and as a result there is often less stress throughout the family.

Communication

The two primary types of communication that members of a family use to communicate with one another are affective communication and instrumental communication. Affective communication is any communication where an individual demonstrates their feelings whether it is through facial expressions, motions, gestures, or even by stating their feelings outright. Instrumental communication is when an individual informs another member of the family of a piece of factual information that is necessary to carry out the normal day-to-day functions of the family such as a mother informing her child where he can find his or her socks. Families that use both types of communication usually function more effectively than families that use instrumental communication more often than affective communication.

Clear communication is when an individual states the information they are trying to convey outright and there can be no question as to the meaning of their statement. For example, if someone were to state "I am upset because Daniel is not home from the movies yet" that is an example of clear communication as there is no question that the individual making the statement is upset and they are specifically upset at Daniel for not being home. On the other hand, masked communication is when an individual states the information they are trying to convey in a vague and perhaps somewhat more confusing manner. For example, if someone were to state simply "I am upset" that would be an example of masked communication as there is no indication to the rest of the family as to exactly why the person is upset. As can be seen through these examples, clear communication is always more effective in conveying a particular piece of information than masked communication

Direct communication is when a person who is attempting to communicate a particular piece of information simply just tells that information to the person they want to receive the information. Indirect communication, on the other hand, is when the person communicating the information states the information, but not to anyone in particular. For example, if a parent told their child "Christine, we need to set the table" that is an example of direct communication as the parent is addressing the person they want to talk to directly. However, if the parent instead simply muttered out loud "we need to set the table" rather than saying it to someone in particular that would be an example of indirect communication. Direct communication is far more effective in carrying out the day-to-day functions necessary to maintain a family than indirect communication because various tasks can be assigned directly to a particular individual.

Families with individuals that use direct, clear communication, listen to the other members of the family, spend more time together communicating, respect each other's points of view, and pay attention to the more subtle forms of affective communication are the most effective. Each individual within the family, by informing the individuals that make up the family directly and concisely of the information they need to convey creates a much more effective form of communication than that which would be found in any other setting. If the individuals receiving the information listen to and respect their fellow family members and often more importantly make the time to listen to them in the first place, the communication between family members will become much stronger. Of course, this communication can be strengthened even further if members of the family are careful to take note of emotional indicators that allow them to realize the feelings of another family member without that person having to actually express their feelings verbally.

Problem-solving steps

A well functioning family would first identify the problem itself and determine exactly what the cause of the problem is.

The family would then come up with a list of solutions that could potentially solve the problem and then attempt to determine the benefits of each solution. After determining the benefits of each solution, the family would choose the solution that seemed to best solve the problem that they had encountered and then, after putting the solution into effect, monitor the solution to make sure that it actually solved the problem. Finally, the family would decide whether the solution worked or not to determine whether it was necessary to try something else. This entire process is important to the functioning of a family as it prevents problems from being misdiagnosed early on and prevents them from getting too far out of control.

Conflict

The causes of conflict within a relationship are too numerous to mention all of them, but some of the common causes include: setting expectations that are too high, not appreciating or respecting the other person in the relationship, not considering the feelings of the other person in the relationship, being afraid of showing affection or emotion, being over-dependent on the other member of the relationship, being inflexible, expecting the other member of the relationship to change, a lack of effective communication, etc... Preventing conflict can be extremely difficult and preventing it altogether is virtually impossible, but avoiding some or all of these common sources can greatly reduce the number of conflicts that take place in any given relationship.

A family that is attempting to resolve a conflict can prevent the conflict from getting out of control and bring it closer to a successful resolution by following steps very similar to that of the basic problem-solving model. First, the family needs to attempt to identify the problem making sure to keep communication between the members of the family open, objective, and with as little hostility as possible. Once the problem is identified then the family needs to attempt to recognize the various positions that each member of the family has regarding the conflict while again attempting to keep hostility to a minimum. After each person involved in the conflict has made their position clear, the family needs to attempt to find a compromise that will work for everyone involved. Each step of the conflict resolution process requires that the people involved in the conflict remain as patient and as understanding as possible, which can often be extremely difficult especially when a solution or compromise cannot be determined immediately.

Social interaction

Outside social interaction is extremely important for every member of a family, regardless of age, as it offers an opportunity for each individual to improve their social skills, educate themselves about the world around them, and learn more about values that one might not learn from the family alone. This is especially true in the case of children as research shows that children who have regular outside social interaction, through things such as extracurricular activities, are less likely to rebel and cause problems and more likely to do better in school and relationships. Outside social interaction is also necessary for the children of a family to eventually leave the household and create a family of their own as they need to seek out their own relationships. Therefore, social interaction with individuals outside of the family is necessary not only for the fulfillment of the members of the family, but to continue the lifecycle of the family as well.

Human Development Education and Services

Changing roles

Fifty to sixty years ago women were the primary caretakers of the family's children and in charge of maintaining the household while the men worked to provide for the family. This has changed, however, due to the drastic increase in the number of women entering the work force since that time, which is partially due to the fact that it has become progressively more difficult for families to live off of one income alone. Both members of the marital couple are often forced to work to provide for the family, which can make it difficult when trying to balance the responsibilities of caretaker and provider. Men, who were once the primary providers for the family, are still out in the workforce, but their spouses have joined them as well and both individuals have to find ways to make the time to care for the children of the family.

Nature versus nurture

The concept of nature vs. nurture is simply the idea that out of all of the traits that any given individual has, some are a result of their genetic heritage and some are a result of their environment. Nature in this context refers to any trait that an individual is born with and that they acquired through genes passed down from their parents. Nurture is in some ways seen as the opposite of nature as it refers to any trait that an individual learns from the environment around them. Nurture often refers to specifically the environment created by the parents of the child, but it can refer to any

environmental condition that affects the development of that child. The concept of nature vs. nurture is important because it shows that individuals inherit some of their traits from their parents, but they also develop many of their traits from their environment.

Genetic and environmental traits

Some examples of traits that researchers have proven to be almost completely genetic and therefore linked to genes passed on from a child's parents to the child are eye color, blood type, most diseases and in most cases the risk of future diseases, vision and vision impairments, etc... Religion and language, on the other hand, are examples of traits that researchers have proven to be almost completely environmental. These traits are all linked to specific genes or to specific environmental factors, but most traits are actually a result of both environmental and genetic influence. Traits such as height, weight, and skin color are all examples of traits that are influenced by both an individual's genes and their environment.

Dvelopmental task concept

The developmental task concept is a theory of human development established by Robert Havinghurst that states that there are certain tasks that each individual needs to go through at certain points during their life to continue developing into a happy and successful adult. These tasks are separated into three groups by their causes and are tasks that are a result of physical maturation, personal causes, and societal pressures. A child learning to crawl is an example of a task that becomes necessary as the child matures physically while an individual learning basic first aid because they are interested in becoming an EMT is a personal cause. While a child that needs to learn how to behave appropriately in a store is an example of a task that would be presented as a result of a societal pressure.

The major age periods that Havinghurst identified for his developmental task concept are:

- Infancy and early childhood is the period from ages 0 to 5 and consists of tasks such as learning to walk and talk, learning to eat solid foods, and learning right from wrong.
- Middle childhood is the period of development from ages 6 to 12 and includes tasks such as learning to get along with others, learning moral values, and learning skills and knowledge required for day-to-day living.
- Adolescence is the period from ages 13 to 18 and requires tasks that include learning how to relate with members of the opposite sex, learning the social role of your gender in society, and preparing for life after childhood.
- Early adulthood is the period of life from ages 19 to 29 and is the age range where tasks such as starting a long-term relationship, finding a career, and starting a family are required.
- Middle adulthood is the period from ages 30 to 60 and includes tasks such as finding adult recreational activities, making achievements in your chosen career, and helping your teenage children to become healthy and happy adults.
- Later maturity is the period from ages 61 to the end of a person's life and consists of tasks such as adjusting to the death of a spouse, adjusting to the effects of old age, and finding people your own age to interact with.

Erik Erikson

Erik Erikson's theory of psychosocial development breaks the process of human development into eight stages that each person needs to pass during their life to continue functioning in a healthy fashion. The eight stages Erikson identified are infancy, younger years, early childhood, middle childhood, adolescence, early adulthood, middle adulthood, and later adulthood. During each of these stages, each individual has to overcome a particular obstacle to their development, which Erikson called a crisis, to be able to continue developing and face the crises of later stages. If an individual were not able to overcome one of the crises along the way, later crises would be more difficult to overcome as well. Erikson's theory also indicated that individuals who were unable to pass through a particular crisis successfully would likely encounter that same crisis again later in life.

- The first stage of Erikson's theory of psychosocial development is infancy and this stage covers the range of time from birth to 12 months. In this stage, the child is presented with the crisis of trust vs. mistrust. Even though everyone struggles with this crisis throughout their lives, the child needs to be able to realize the concept of trust and realize elements of certainty such as the fact that if the child's parents leave the room, they aren't going to abandon the child forever. If the child is unable to realize that there are certain things that can be left to trust because, for example, the child actually is abandoned, the child may become withdrawn and avoid interaction with the rest of society.
- The second stage of Erikson's theory of psychosocial

development is the younger years stage, which covers the range of years from ages 1 to 3. In this stage, the child is faced with the crisis of autonomy vs. shame and doubt and is presented with the need to become independent and learn skills such as using the toilet without assistance. If the child is able to overcome this crisis, the child will gain a sense of self-pride that is necessary to continue fostering the child's growing need for independence as he or she gets older. If, however, the child is unable to overcome this crisis and cannot establish his or her own independence, the child will develop feelings of shame and doubt about the child's ability to function without assistance.

- The third stage of Erikson's theory of psychosocial development is the early childhood stage, which covers the range of time from ages 3 to 5. In this stage, the child is faced with the crisis of initiative vs. guilt and is presented with the need to discover the ambition necessary to continue functioning independently and ultimately a sense of the person the child wants to become in the future. This stage is strongly linked with the moral development of the child as he or she begins to use make-believe play to explore the kind of person he or she wants to become. If the child is unable to explore their ambitions or is expected to function with too much self-control the child will develop feelings of guilt as the child begins to see their ambitions, dreams, and goals as unattainable or inappropriate.

- The fourth stage of Erikson's theory of psychosocial development is the middle childhood stage, which covers ages 6 to 10. In this stage, the child is faced with the crisis of industry vs. inferiority and is presented with the need to develop the ability to complete productive tasks, such as schoolwork, and work together in groups with other people. If the child is unable to learn how to work effectively, either alone or in a group, the child will develop a sense of inferiority as a result of their inability to complete the tasks set before them that the child's peers are capable of completing. For example, if a child is regularly unable to complete their homework because the child does not understand the material while the rest of the child's peers are not having difficulty, this can lead the child to develop a sense of inferiority.

- The fifth stage of Erikson's theory of psychosocial development is the adolescence stage, which covers ages 11 to 18. In this stage, the child is faced with the crisis of identity vs. role confusion where the child attempts to find his or her place in society and determine his or her future goals and the skills and values necessary to achieve those goals. It is also at this stage that the child becomes more aware of how the people around the child perceive him or her and begins to become concerned with those perceptions. If the child is unable to determine what future goals he or she is interested in pursuing, it can lead to confusion about what roles the child will play once the child reaches adulthood.

- The sixth stage of Erikson's theory of psychosocial development is the early adulthood stage, which covers ages 18 to 34. In this stage, the young adult is concerned with the crisis of intimacy vs. isolation where the individual needs to begin establishing intimate relationships with others. If the adult is unable to form intimate relationships with other individuals, perhaps because of disappointments regarding relationships earlier in life, the individual will become more withdrawn and isolate themselves from others. Isolation can prove to be a dangerous problem to the development of a healthy adult as it not only prevents the individual from forming lasting relationships, but the lack of social interaction can lead to severe personality flaws, which may hinder any future attempts at developing relationships later in life.
- The seventh stage of Erikson's theory of psychosocial development is the middle adulthood stage and occurs between ages 35 to 60. In this stage, the adult becomes aware of the crisis of generativity vs. stagnation where the individual is concerned with continuing their genetic line before it is too late. Generativity refers to the ability to produce offspring and then nurture, guide, and prepare that offspring for future life. At the same time, however, generativity in this context also refers to any act that gives something of value, such as teaching children how to read, to the next generation. If an individual is unable to contribute to the next generation in some form or another, the individual will feel a sense of failure that is a result of stagnation, which is simply a lack of accomplishment.
- The last stage of Erikson's eight stages of psychosocial development is the later adulthood stage, which is the period starting at age 60 that goes on to the end of the individual's life. In the later adulthood stage, the individual is confronted with the crisis of ego integrity vs. despair where the adult begins to examine the course of his or her life and ultimately the kind of person that he or she has been over the years. If the adult feels that he or she has had a meaningful life and has accomplished something during it, this will lead to a strong sense of integrity. However, if the adult is unhappy with the way that the individual acted during his or her life, they will fall into a sense of despair as the individual begins to fear death and the absolute end of any chance of achieving anything further.

Jean Piaget

Jean Piaget's theory of cognitive development theorizes that a child will learn more effectively if the child is allowed to actively adapt to the world around them through their own play and exploration rather than being taught skills and knowledge by other people. Piaget's theory suggests that during a child's development there are four major stages that the child will go through as they begin to acquire new skills that will aid their ability to learn and process information on their own. The four stages that Piaget identifies are the sensorimotor stage, which lasts from ages 0 to 2, the preoperational stage for ages 2 to 7, the concrete operational stage for ages 7 to 11, and the formal operational stage for ages 11 and onward. Piaget's theory is important to the study of child development as it was the first theory that actually recognized the concept that children can actively and effectively learn on their own rather than having to gain knowledge from simply being taught by another person.

- The first stage of Piaget's theory of cognitive development, the sensorimotor stage, lasts from birth to age 2 and is the period where a child uses their senses of sight, hearing, and touch to learn about and explore elements of the world around them. Through a combination of these senses, a child is able to discover new ways of solving simple problems such as how to move their hands to drop a block into a bucket and removing it again or using their eyes to find an object or person that has been hidden. As a result, it is also at this stage that the child begins to develop their hand-eye coordination and an ability to reason out a method of achieving any given goal.
- The second stage of Piaget's theory of cognitive development, the preoperational stage, lasts from ages 2 to 7 and is the stage where children begin to use words, symbols, and pictures to describe what they have discovered about particular elements of the world around them. This stage is where children begin to develop an understanding of language and can focus their attention on a particular subject or object rather than everything going on at once. However, Piaget theorized that children at this stage of development also have a faulty sense of logic when attempting to understand certain concepts such as volume, mass, and number when some element of what they perceived was changed. For example, if a liquid was poured into a tall container and than an equal amount of liquid was poured into a smaller, but wider container, the children would believe that the taller container contained more liquid even though this obviously was not the case.
- The third stage of Piaget's theory of cognitive development, the concrete operational stage, which takes place between ages 7 and 11, is the stage where a child's thinking becomes more logical regarding concrete concepts. For example, in this stage children are now capable of understanding concepts of mass, volume, and number and are able to realize that two containers of different shapes that each have the same amount of liquid poured into them still contain the same amount of liquid. The child will also begin to learn how to identify and organize objects according to their shape, size, color, and so on. The child, however, will still not be able to understand more abstract concepts, such as what you might find in calculus or algebra, until they reach the formal operational stage of development.
- The fourth and final stage of Piaget's theory of cognitive development, the formal operational stage, starts at age 11 and continues until the end of the individual's life. This stage is where an individual begins to understand more abstract concepts and develops a logical way of thinking about those concepts. In other words, the

individual begins to understand ideas that are less concrete or absolute and cannot necessarily be backed up by physical evidence or observation such as morality, advanced mathematics, and a person's state of being. It is also within this stage of development that individuals become able to understand all of the variables in a problem and are able to determine most if not all of the possible solutions to the problem rather than just the solutions that are most obvious. This stage is never truly completed, but rather continues throughout a person's life as the individual continues to develop and improve on their ability to think abstractly.

Later researchers have challenged Piaget's theory of cognitive development because studies indicate that Piaget may have underestimated the abilities of younger children to learn and understand various concepts. Piaget's theory indicates that younger children are unable to understand certain concrete and abstract thoughts early within their development even if another individual taught the child. However, this has actually been disproved as research shows that children of a young age can actually be taught how to handle and understand problems that Piaget believed only older children would be able to comprehend. Researchers have also challenged Piaget's theory because studies indicate that if a younger child is given a task like one an older child might receive, but the difficulty of the task is adjusted to compensate for age, the child would actually be able to more effectively understand the concept. Piaget's theory is still important because it presents the importance of active learning in a child's development, but it also ignores many of the benefits of adult teaching.

Abraham Maslow

Abraham Maslow originally theorized that there were five types of human needs that form a sort of pyramid if they are arranged in order of their importance. Maslow also stated that no individual would be able to focus on the upper layers of the pyramid until they were able to meet the needs presented at the layers below first.

- The first layer of the pyramid is the layer that contains the physiological needs, which are the basic needs required for the individual's survival such as food, water, breathable air, sleep, etc…
- The second layer of the pyramid is the layer that contains the safety needs, which are the elements that the individual needs to feel a sense of security such as having a job, good health, and a safe place to live.
- The third layer of the pyramid is the layer that contains the love and belonging needs, which is the basic need to form social relationships such as those with friends, family, and intimate loved ones.
- The fourth layer of the five layers of the pyramid that makes up Maslow's hierarchy of human needs is the esteem layer, which contains the individual's need to respect him or herself and others as well as the need to be respected and accepted by others.
- The fifth and top layer of the pyramid is the self-actuation layer of the pyramid and contains the individual's need for morality, creativity, and trust. Maslow theorized that individuals could survive without reaching the later levels of the pyramid, but they would feel a sense of anxiousness if the needs of the later levels

were not met. Maslow also believed that individuals who reached the later levels of the pyramid did not receive any tangible benefit from meeting the needs of those layers other than a feeling of fulfillment and the motivation to fulfill needs higher on the pyramid.

Maslow later added two additional layers above the self-actuation layer of the pyramid, which are the cognitive layer and the aesthetic layer.
- The cognitive layer is the layer that contains an individual's need to acquire and ultimately understand both abstract and concrete knowledge.
- The aesthetic layer, which became the final layer in later versions of the pyramid, is the layer that presents the individual's need to discover, create, and experience beauty and art.

Maslow also later theorized that if an individual was unable to meet the needs of the any given layer of the pyramid that those needs could become neurotic needs, which are compulsions that if satisfied would not aid in the individual's health and growth in any fashion.

Intervention and giftedness

Early childhood intervention is the process by which children who are experiencing developmental difficulties or showing signs of difficulties are diagnosed and treated as early as possible to allow them to continue developing in the best manner that the child can. Early childhood intervention services usually take place before the child reaches school age because studies indicate that the earlier a child who is experiencing difficulties receives special education, the

more effective that education will ultimately be.

Children who possess intellectual giftedness are children that are born with a significantly higher than average IQ and are capable of learning concepts and information much more quickly than other children of their age. Even though intellectual giftedness is an asset to the child, the child often requires education that is adjusted for the speed that the child can learn at or the child will become bored, frustrated, isolated, and actually even begin to underachieve.

Substance abuse

Substance abuse is a disorder where an individual begins to overuse or becomes dependent upon a particular drug or a group of drugs that ultimately has a negative impact on the health of the individual. Substance abuse, especially when the individual using the drug becomes addicted or dependent on the drug, can affect the individual's ability to interact both socially and physically, and abilities such as their ability to communicate intelligibly with other people or even to complete relatively simple tasks can be severely hindered. Once an individual becomes chemically dependent on a particular drug, there body actually develops a physical need for the drug and the individual will experience the effects of withdrawal if they are unable to meet that need. However, substance abuse not only affects a person by causing health problems, but also can severely hinder an individual's ability for social development, as the individual often has difficulty improving on social skills due to his or her inability to control behavior, actions, and even basic speech.

Teenage pregnancy

Teenage pregnancy, which can be defined as the act of a woman expecting a child prior to her 20th birthday or in some areas prior to her being considered a legal adult, can have a large number of physical, social, economic, and psychological effects. Studies show that women who become pregnant as teenagers have a significantly higher chance of giving birth to the child prematurely, a higher risk of the child being born at an unhealthy weight, and a higher risk of complications during pregnancy, especially when the mother is under age 15. It has also been shown that teenage mothers are more likely to drop out of high school and even more likely never to finish college, which can make it much more difficult for a teenage mother to find a job, especially if she is the sole caretaker of the child. Children born to teenage mothers have also been shown to be at higher risk for behavioral problems and often have more difficulty functioning in school.

The two primary ways that the risk of teenage pregnancy can be reduced are through the promotion of contraceptive use or abstinence and the promotion of social interaction between the teenager and her parents. The best way to reduce the risk of teenage pregnancy is certainly not to have intercourse at all, but the use of a contraceptive, even though it does not guarantee that a teenager will not become pregnant, can greatly reduce the chances of pregnancy when used correctly. Studies have also shown that teenagers that have regular open communication with their parents are more likely to wait to have intercourse until later in their lives. However, regardless of what precautions are used, the risk of teenage pregnancy cannot be eliminated completely as there is always the risk of contraceptives failing or the risk that the teenager may be the victim of a rape.

The most important thing for a young mother to continue functioning and raise her child in a healthy fashion is that she is able to maintain a stable and effective support system both before and after the child is born. Studies have shown that most of the physical effects that teenage pregnancy has upon the child, when the mother becomes pregnant at age 15 or older, are a result of malnutrition and poor prenatal care. Both of these factors can be greatly reduced or eliminated if the young mother has help from parents or outside resources that teach her what to eat and where to get appropriate care. A strong support system is also essential in aiding the mother financially and in actually raising the child as teenage parents almost always lack the resources and the life experience necessary to both supply and care for the child.

Teenage suicide

There are a large number of factors that can increase the risk of a teenager committing suicide, but studies indicate that the teenager's history, emotional and physical health, social pressures, and access to the equipment necessary to carry out the suicide are the most likely to have a role. If the teenager has attempted to commit suicide previously, has a history of drug or alcohol abuse, has a history of depression or other mental illness, or another member of his or her family has committed suicide or been abused, the teenager's risk of suicide increases. Physical illness, religious or cultural pressures, and other suicides in the community can also lead to an increased risk of suicide. Finally, if the teenager has access to guns, knives, drugs, or any other means of taking his or her own life, the teenager may be at heightened risk for suicide as well.

Teenage suicide can be difficult to prevent, but identifying the risk factors and attempting to minimize their effects before they are allowed to escalate is the most effective way to prevent teenage suicide. Teenagers that do not have access to the instruments necessary to easily commit suicide, but have access to facilities for both mental and physical health and support that promotes the use of such facilities, and overall have strong family, societal, and religious support are much less likely to commit suicide. Teenagers who have been taught methods of solving problems and conflicts in a non-violent fashion by their parents or teachers have also been shown to be at a much lower risk of suicide as well.

Practice Test

Practice Questions

1. The process through which a person comes to think of himself or herself as a distinct person despite being a member of a family is known as
   a. collectivization.
   b. individuation.
   c. personalization.
   d. ego birth.
   e. personification.

2. In which kind of society are people more likely to live with their extended families?
   a. Modern
   b. Industrial
   c. Urban
   d. Agrarian
   e. Nomadic

3. Which of the following is NOT considered to be necessary for a person to commit emotionally to a marriage?
   a. Good self-esteem
   b. Empathy
   c. A feeling of permanence
   d. Financial stability
   e. A strong personal identity

4. Which of the following factors has no effect on job satisfaction?
   a. Having a child between the ages of 2 and 4
   b. Flexible scheduling
   c. Parenting a newborn
   d. High wages
   e. Intellectual challenge

5. What is the first step a person should take after divorce?
   a. Receive justice from the former spouse
   b. Achieve balance between being single and being a parent
   c. Accept the fact that the marriage is over
   d. Develop goals for the future
   e. Begin looking for a new partner

6. For which pair would sibling rivalry likely be greatest?
    a. Sister and brother, ages 5 and 10, respectively
    b. Sisters, ages 10 and 5
    c. Brother and sister, ages 8 and 10, respectively
    d. Brothers, ages 3 and 5
    e. Sisters, ages 4 and 8

7. Which of the following statements about marriage is false?
    a. Married men are less likely to abuse alcohol.
    b. Married women typically earn higher wages than single women.
    c. On average, married women are healthier than single women.
    d. People who have been married in the past are more likely to marry again than people who have never married.
    e. More than 90% of Americans will marry at some point.

8. In general, accepting a stepparent is hardest for
    a. preschoolers.
    b. girls around the age of eight.
    c. boys around the age of nine.
    d. adolescent boys.
    e. adolescent girls.

9. Which of the following statements about families is false?
    a. The content rather than the style of family communication is important.
    b. Families tend to make decisions that maintain the current state of affairs.
    c. Members of a family are likely to struggle with the same sorts of problems in life.
    d. Families change in response to pressures from the environment.
    e. It is impossible to understand the members of a family without understanding the family as a whole.

10. According to John Gottman, which of the following is the best response to criticism by a spouse?
    a. Defensiveness
    b. Stonewalling
    c. Reasoned argument
    d. Humor
    e. Acceptance

11. The greatest amount of variation between people of the same age is found during
    a. Infancy
    b. Early adolescence
    c. Early childhood
    d. Adulthood
    e. Late adolescence

12. When two children have a dispute and agree to settle it according to their mother's opinion, they are engaging in
   a. Arbitration
   b. Conciliation
   c. Mediation
   d. Negotiation
   e. Restorative justice

13. In general, when a mother works,
   a. her daughters are less independent.
   b. her unsupervised sons are less successful at school.
   c. her children have more self-esteem.
   d. it is not important for both parents to have a positive attitude about the arrangement.
   e. she is less satisfied with her life.

14. Which of the following is an assumption of structured family therapy?
   a. The life of a family is a series of actions and reactions.
   b. Family members tend to become locked in their roles.
   c. During times of conflict, family members will take sides to consolidate power.
   d. Bad behavior persists when it is reinforced.
   e. Family problems are caused by negative projection.

15. What is one drawback of inpatient treatment for alcoholism?
   a. It is rarely effective.
   b. It does not include a twelve-step program.
   c. It enables the patient to continue drinking while receiving treatment.
   d. It is expensive.
   e. It requires a personal commitment from the patient.

16. According to Piaget's model, the ability to imagine the mental lives of others emerges during the
   a. formal operational stage.
   b. concrete operational stage.
   c. primary socialization stage.
   d. preoperational stage.
   e. sensorimotor stage.

17. Role strain is exemplified by
   a. a public speaker who cultivates her expertise.
   b. a new teacher who struggles to maintain authority in the classroom.
   c. a person whose parents die.
   d. a child who imagines what it would be like to be a police officer.
   e. a substitute teacher who waits tables on the weekend.

18. Which of the following people is most likely to have an IQ of 125?
    a. A fourteen year-old with the mental age of a ten year-old
    b. A five year-old with the mental age of an eight year-old
    c. A ten year-old with the mental age of a seven year-old
    d. An eight year-old with the mental age of a twelve year-old
    e. An eight year-old with the mental age of a ten year-old

19. A student whose interest level and performance have steadily declined admits to his teacher that he is depressed. Unfortunately, the student is not yet willing to do anything to remedy this problem. In which stage of the transtheoretical model of change is this student?
    a. Action
    b. Maintenance
    c. Preparation/commitment
    d. Contemplation
    e. Precontemplation

20. Starting at about nine months, an infant will begin nonsensically imitating adult speech, a process known as
    a. telegraphic speech.
    b. holophrastic speech.
    c. cooing.
    d. deep structuring.
    e. echolalia.

21. What is the major criticism of Levinson's "seasons" of life model?
    a. It overstates the importance of the mid-life crisis.
    b. It is too idealized.
    c. It ignores the last years of life.
    d. It suggests that life transitions are made unconsciously.
    e. It discounts the influence of parents.

22. Which of the following is NOT a warning sign of teen depression?
    a. Sudden interest in a new hobby
    b. Aloofness
    c. Fatigue
    d. A change in sleep patterns
    e. Rapid weight change

23. Students who excel in math receive different treatment than students who excel in English. This is an example of
    a. vertical socialization.
    b. horizontal socialization.
    c. resocialization.
    d. anticipatory socialization.
    e. desocialization.

24. Which of the following is NOT one of the areas of emotional intelligence?
    a. Self-awareness
    b. Empathy
    c. Personal motivation
    d. Thrift
    e. Altruism

25. Which of the following statements about teen pregnancy is false?
    a. The United States has the lowest rate of teen pregnancy in North America.
    b. The rate of teen pregnancy is higher among Hispanics and African-Americans.
    c. Teenage mothers are less likely to complete high school.
    d. Teen pregnancy rates have decreased over the past twenty years.
    e. Teenage parents earn less money over the course of their lives.

26. An effective time management plan
    a. encourages students to do their most difficult tasks first.
    b. eliminates every possible distraction.
    c. includes time for meals.
    d. eschews lists.
    e. will be the same for every student.

27. Creating a list of things to do is less necessary
    a. when children are teething.
    b. when both parents work in the home.
    c. when a daily routine has been established.
    d. when children are in school.
    e. when both parents work outside the home.

28. Which of Hersey and Blanchard's leadership styles emphasizes the performance of tasks and ignores the development of positive relationships?
    a. Selling
    b. Delegating
    c. Supporting
    d. Telling
    e. Participating

29. What is the best method for a family to decide on a vacation destination?
    a. One parent decides
    b. Ideas are thrown into a hat and selected at random
    c. Children decide
    d. Discussion, then a final decision by parents
    e. Vote

30. The best way to limit a child's television time is to
    a. take away privileges until the child submits.
    b. tell the child that television will rot his brain.
    c. ignore the issue.
    d. suggest that the child go outside.
    e. set a timer and turn the television off when the alarm sounds.

31. A group will often make more extreme decisions than any one member would make independently. This phenomenon is known as
    a. organizational conflict.
    b. group polarization.
    c. social facilitation.
    d. groupthink.
    e. social loafing.

32. The members of a family are more likely to be motivated when
    a. they are forced to commit to a goal.
    b. a goal is well defined.
    c. they believe that their work is inherently good, regardless of any tangible reward.
    d. they do not evaluate their own performance.
    e. they feel as if they are working harder than other members.

33. A compressed workweek
    a. decreases the amount of time spent at work every day.
    b. is made up of 5 eight-hour days.
    c. improves employee satisfaction.
    d. tends to diminish performance.
    e. is especially beneficial for employees who work at home.

34. What is the first step a person should take toward eliminating wasted time?
    a. Keeping a log of how time is spent
    b. Resolving to sleep less
    c. Purchasing efficient home appliances
    d. Using an egg timer
    e. Focusing on one's most important tasks

35. A five year-old is probably too young to
    a. clean up spills with a sponge.
    b. sweep a wooden floor.
    c. dust shelves.
    d. mop the kitchen floor.
    e. put away toys.

36. The proper decision-making process begins by
    a. defining the problem to be solved.
    b. listing various solutions.
    c. researching potential solutions.
    d. assembling a team to solve the problem.
    e. estimating the cost of solving the problem.

37. When making a schedule, children should be encouraged to
      I. include some free time.
      II. place the hardest tasks first.
      III. block out long stretches for completing all homework.
    a. I only
    b. II only
    c. III only
    d. I and II
    e. II and III

38. Drop-in child care is useful when
    a. parents have very little money.
    b. a family's regular child care provider is unavailable.
    c. a family is away from home.
    d. a child has special needs.
    e. a child is in school.

39. What is one disadvantage of dealing with consumer finance companies?
    a. They do not loan money for very many purposes.
    b. They provide different rates of interest depending on the client's credit record.
    c. They help consumers purchase goods they could not otherwise afford.
    d. They tend to charge high interest rates.
    e. They do not accept property as security.

40. What type of business is the most common employer of high-school students?
    a. Grocery stores
    b. Movie theaters
    c. Theme parks
    d. Clothing stores
    e. Restaurants

41. Borrowers with a poor credit rating will not be eligible for a bank's
    a. prime rate.
    b. savings deposits.
    c. demand deposits.
    d. deposit insurance.
    e. certificates of deposit.

42. Which of the following statements about daycare is true?
    a. Children in daycare tend to be less aggressive.
    b. It is not necessary to establish the parent-child bond before beginning daycare.
    c. Children not in daycare tend to make friends more easily.
    d. The value of daycare is not related to the quality of the supervision.
    e. Children in daycare are better at articulating their desires.

43. Which of the following was NOT one of the consumer rights asserted by Presidents Kennedy and Nixon during the 1960s?
    a. Right to a safe product
    b. Right to affordability
    c. Right to redress
    d. Right to be heard
    e. Right to be informed

44. According to personal finance experts, what is the maximum percentage of income a family should spend on housing?
    a. 5%
    b. 50%
    c. 10%
    d. 25%
    e. 35%

45. Which of the following represents a discretionary expense?
    a. Textbook
    b. Rent
    c. DVD
    d. Groceries
    e. Heating oil

46. What is the typical interval for a personal budget?
    a. One day
    b. One week
    c. One month
    d. Six months
    e. One year

47. Denise has a credit card with an APR of 4.5%. If she has an average balance of $2500 throughout the year, how much interest will accrue?
    a. $25.00
    b. $112.50
    c. $450.00
    d. $450.50
    e. $2612.50

48. It is NOT a good idea to
    a. allow a child to visit a daycare center before his or her first official day there.
    b. ask daycare providers how toilet training is handled.
    c. allow a child to bring his favorite blanket or stuffed animal to daycare.
    d. visit less than three daycare providers before selecting one.
    e. have a positive discussion with a child who is about to begin daycare.

49. Which type of corporate bond is secured only by the assets and earnings of the corporation?
    a. Collateral trust bond
    b. Mortgage bond
    c. Sinking-fund bond
    d. Convertible bond
    e. Debenture bond

50. What is the major benefit of vitamin A?
    a. It helps form new cells.
    b. It helps protect the body from disease.
    c. It can increase a person's concentration and alertness.
    d. It can give a person healthy hair and skin.
    e. It enables muscle contraction.

51. From which food group should the most daily servings be taken?
    a. Bread, cereal, rice, and pasta
    b. Milk, yogurt, and cheese
    c. Fats, oils, and sweets
    d. Vegetables
    e. Meat, poultry, fish, eggs, dry beans, and nuts

52. The daily values listed on food packaging assume that
    a. the food will be shared between two people.
    b. the food will not be cooked.
    c. a person's daily diet consists of two thousand calories.
    d. the product contains preservatives.
    e. the product is unspoiled.

53. In order to reduce the risk of spinal bifida in infants, food manufacturers have begun adding
    a. calcium.
    b. folic acid.
    c. iron.
    d. vitamin K.
    e. magnesium.

54. Which of the following events decreases metabolism?
    a. Rapid weight loss
    b. Increase in muscle mass
    c. Slow weight gain
    d. Moderate workout
    e. Rapid weight gain

55. An ovo-lacto-vegetarian is a person who eats
    a. Fruits, vegetables, and grains
    b. Fruits, vegetables, grains, and poultry
    c. Fruits, vegetables, grains, and dairy products
    d. Fruits, vegetables, grains, dairy products, and eggs
    e. Fruits, vegetables, grains, and eggs

56. Sodium and chloride are major minerals; every day a person should consume ___ of each.
    a. 100 milligrams
    b. 1 kilogram
    c. 10 milligrams
    d. 10 grams
    e. 1 gram

57. Which of the following vitamins is water-soluble?
    a. Vitamin D
    b. Vitamin E
    c. Vitamin K
    d. Vitamin A
    e. Vitamin C

58. What is one problem associated with the over-consumption of protein?
    a. Dehydration
    b. Increased muscle mass
    c. Strained liver and kidneys
    d. Heart palpitations
    e. Dandruff

59. Which kind of oil is NOT an unsaturated fat?
    a. Corn oil
    b. Olive oil
    c. Canola oil
    d. Palm oil
    e. Sunflower oil

60. The amount of energy required to raise the temperature of one gram of water by one degree Celsius is a(n)
    a. joule.
    b. calorie.
    c. ohm.
    d. microgram.
    e. watt.

61. A person who is 41 to 100% heavier than his or her ideal weight is
    a. mildly obese.
    b. osteoporotic.
    c. diabetic.
    d. moderately obese.
    e. severely obese.

62. Which of the following statements is true?
        I. Bulimia can lead to tooth decay.
        II. Anorexics tend to have a distorted self-image.
        III. Bulimia does not always include purging.
    a. I only
    b. II only
    c. III only
    d. I and II only
    e. I, II, and III

63. Which nutrient is not present in high levels in dairy products?
    a. Vitamin B-12
    b. Iron
    c. Protein
    d. Vitamin A
    e. Calcium

64. Which of the following vitamins is known to improve the body's ability to use phosphorus and calcium?
    a. Vitamin E
    b. Vitamin D
    c. Vitamin B-3
    d. Vitamin K
    e. Vitamin A

65. Which of the following statements about stain removal is true?
    a. Stained garments can be safely ironed.
    b. A fresh stain can be cleaned with bar soap.
    c. Milk stains should be treated with hot water.
    d. Regular clothing can be washed alongside clothing with chemical stains.
    e. Stained clothing should be cleaned within 24 hours.

66. Which fabrication method, typical of outerwear, involves stitching a liner fabric in between two outer fabrics?
    a. Knitting
    b. Stitch-through
    c. Quilting
    d. Tufting
    e. Weaving

67. What is the name for wool that has been spun into a fine yarn from parallel threads?
    a. Worsted
    b. Cashmere
    c. Angora
    d. Polyester
    e. Spandex

68. Fuzzy fibers that ball up and adhere to the outside of a garment are said to be
    a. fuzzing.
    b. snagging.
    c. breathing.
    d. pilling.
    e. creasing.

69. What does the word *carded* mean when it appears on a clothing label?
    a. The garment has been evaluated by a licensed inspector.
    b. The garment is made of short and thick cotton fibers.
    c. The garment was not created in a sweat shop.
    d. The garment only contains one type of fiber.
    e. The garment is resistant to wrinkles.

70. Which of the following garments would be the most resistant to wrinkles?
    a. Rayon jacket
    b. Cotton t-shirt
    c. Silk shirt
    d. Linen pants
    e. Wool pants

71. What is one common problem with silk clothing?
    a. It is easily damaged by the sun.
    b. It is very susceptible to abrasions.
    c. It has a tendency to wrinkle.
    d. It is very flammable.
    e. It is coarse.

72. The FTC does NOT mandate that clothing labels include
    a. the country of origin.
    b. whether the garment contains mink or rabbit.
    c. an indication of whether wool is new or recycled.
    d. the Registered Identification Number or name of the manufacturer.
    e. each fiber class represented in the item.

73. On which of the following fabrics is it safe to use bleach occasionally?
    a. Spandex
    b. Silk
    c. Cotton
    d. Wool
    e. Cashmere

74. Which fabric is best for blocking sunlight?
    a. Green satin
    b. Black cotton
    c. White cotton
    d. Black satin
    e. Red cotton

75. In interior design, the arrangement of elements in a pattern around some central point is known as
    a. symmetrical balance.
    b. gradation balance.
    c. asymmetrical balance.
    d. harmonic balance.
    e. radial balance.

76. In which layout pattern are spaces arranged along a linear path, with major elements at either end?
    a. Radial layout
    b. Dumbbell layout
    c. Clustered layout
    d. Doughnut layout
    e. Centralized layout

77. Which of the following represents the Fibonacci sequence?
    a. 0, 1, 1, 2, 3, 5...
    b. 0, 1, 2, 4, 8, 16...
    c. 0, 1, 1.5., 2, 2.5...
    d. 0, 1, 3, 6, 9, 12...
    e. 0, 2, 4, 6, 8, 10...

78. Which of the following is considered to be the most important determinant of human comfort in housing?
    a. Relative humidity
    b. Mean radiant temperature
    c. Air temperature
    d. Air quality
    e. Ventilation

79. Fabric hung across the window by a rod that covers either the extreme ends of the window or the entire window is called a
    a. curtain.
    b. louvered shutter.
    c. drapery.
    d. grille.
    e. Roman shade.

80. A kitchen is fourteen feet long and ten feet wide, but it has an adjoining pantry four feet deep and four feet wide. What is the gross area of the kitchen?
    a. 24 square feet
    b. 32 square feet
    c. 140 square feet
    d. 156 square feet
    e. 2240 square feet

81. The synthetic woodwork finish that creates the most durable surface is
    a. lacquer.
    b. polyurethane.
    c. varnish.
    d. vinyl.
    e. polyester.

82. Which of the following is NOT a good strategy for instructing a learning-disabled student?
    a. Breaking a complicated problem into simple steps
    b. Encouraging students to strive for perfection
    c. Establishing a daily routine
    d. Incorporating movement and tactile instruction whenever possible
    e. Delivering abstract concepts through dialogue with students

83. Which of the following is a cognitive objective of consumer science?
    a. Ability to select drapes
    b. Ability to arrange furniture
    c. Ability to load a shopping cart
    d. Ability to restrain consumer impulses
    e. Ability to create a personal budget

84. What is one common criticism of cooperative education programs?
    a. They isolate students from the rest of the academic community.
    b. They do not provide on-the-job training.
    c. They do not help students make career choices.
    d. They separate the business and academic communities.
    e. They decrease student motivation.

85. Which of the following is NOT one of the focuses of Junior Achievement programs at the high school level?
    a. Personal finance
    b. Business and entrepreneurship
    c. Community service
    d. Work preparation
    e. Economics

86. What is the primary focus of the FCCLA?
   a. College admission
   b. Academic achievement
   c. The family
   d. Career advancement
   e. Consumer education

87. A needs assessment for a family and consumer science program should begin with
   a. a gap analysis.
   b. lesson plans.
   c. prioritization.
   d. time management analysis.
   e. a survey of summative assessment results.

88. Which of the following is NOT a necessary component of an effective syllabus?
   a. Grading scale
   b. Mission statement
   c. List of community resources
   d. Clear assessment objectives
   e. Course content

89. A lesson plan calls for students to act out a negotiating scenario in which pairs of students try to settle a hypothetical dispute between a husband and wife over money. Which learning disability might prevent a student from succeeding at this task?
   a. Dyssemia
   b. Apraxia
   c. Dysgraphia
   d. Dyslexia
   e. Visual perception disorder

90. When evaluating Internet research, what is the least important consideration?
   a. Whether the website has an editorial board
   b. The organization that maintains the website
   c. The presence of links to similar websites
   d. The last time the website was updated
   e. An affiliation with the United States government

91. Many high-school students believe that the most important content area in family and consumer science is
   a. housing.
   b. the family.
   c. consumer science.
   d. personal finance.
   e. food and nutrition.

92. The original purpose of family and consumer science education was to
    a. redress social problems such as child labor and the repression of women.
    b. improve women's housekeeping skills.
    c. encourage frugality during the World War II.
    d. reinforce traditional family roles.
    e. encourage the use of household appliances.

93. Which of the following activities would best develop the psychomotor skills of elementary-school students?
    a. Learning to calculate compound interest
    b. Creating a budget for their school wardrobe
    c. Looking up banking terms in the dictionary
    d. Setting up a mock storefront for a retail business
    e. Drawing a picture of their ideal house

94. Name one advantage of large classes.
    a. Close relations between students and teacher
    b. Greater access to resources
    c. Expanded range of teaching methods
    d. Less record-keeping
    e. Greater comfort for the teacher

95. Which of the following is NOT a relevant factor when making changes in the family and consumer sciences curriculum?
    a. Experience
    b. Knowledge
    c. Time
    d. Skill
    e. Expense

96. A teacher is dividing the class up into groups for a project. What is the best way to avoid gender discrimination?
    a. Segregate the groups by gender.
    b. Encourage boys to include girls when making decisions.
    c. Encourage girls to handle tasks related to math.
    d. Be sure each group is comprised of both boys and girls.
    e. Give leadership positions to at least one boy and one girl in each group.

97. The primary determinant of whether a teacher will adopt instructional technology is
    a. estimated cost.
    b. student interest.
    c. perceived usefulness.
    d. the teacher's aptitude.
    e. geographic location.

98. The Carl D. Perkins Improvement Act of 2006 mandated that
    a. children with disabilities be given a free lunch.
    b. the curriculum of family and consumer science be aligned with general content standards.
    c. family and consumer science teachers obtain an undergraduate degree.
    d. students in family and consumer sciences pass a written examination.
    e. family and consumer sciences teachers focus on career training.

99. An activity that requires students to describe their ideal home falls within the
    a. psychomotor domain.
    b. analytic domain.
    c. cognitive domain.
    d. affective domain.
    e. synthetic domain.

100. Children between the ages of six and eight should be able to
    a. make change.
    b. compare the prices of products.
    c. maintain spending records.
    d. use the terminology associated with banking.
    e. count coins.

Answer Key and Explanations

1. B: Individuation is the process through which a person comes to think of himself or herself as a distinct person despite membership in a family. The development of children in a family can be seen as an ongoing process of individuation. Children at first identify entirely with the mores, norms, and values of their family; it is only after prolonged exposure to other people outside the home that a child will begin to question his or her upbringing and perhaps modify his or her belief system. A fully individualized person is able to maintain a coherent personality without necessarily renouncing membership in a family with which he or she may have some disagreement.

2. D: People who live in an agrarian society are more likely to live with their extended family. An extended family is comprised of more than one adult couple. For instance, it might include a man and a woman, their children, and their grandchildren. Agrarian societies in which people tend the same land for their entire lives are more conducive to the maintenance of the extended family. This is in part because it is more difficult for a large group to move around together. In modern, industrial, urban, and nomadic societies, it is more common for people to be grouped together in nuclear families. A nuclear family includes one adult couple and their children.

3. D: Financial stability is not one of the factors necessary for a person to commit emotionally to a marriage. This fact is interesting, since money is one of the main issues leading many divorces. However, many experts agree that it is much more important for partners to have good self-esteem, empathy, a feeling of permanence in the relationship, and strong personal identities. Solid marriages weather the inevitable hard times with a mixture of humor, empathy, and habit. The idea of empathy is particularly important in marriage because it implies that each partner may not fully understand the other. Nevertheless, a loving spouse will try to help whenever possible.

4. A: Having a young child has no measurable effect on job satisfaction. Curiously, this is true for both men and women. Research suggests that parents often feel some strain as they occupy multiple roles, but this is offset by the enjoyment they derive from their work. Having a newborn, on the other hand, has a noticeably damaging effect on job satisfaction. The demands of caring for a newborn, as well as the desire to spend as much time as possible with this new child, make it unpleasant to be away from home for any reason. Flexible scheduling, high wages, and intellectual challenge are all directly correlated with job satisfaction.

5. C: After divorce, the first step a person should take is to accept that the divorce is final and the marriage is over. This is easier said than done, as psychologists estimate that it takes most people at least two years to accept divorce entirely. Until this is reached, the divorcee should not initiate a new relationship. The best way to complete the process of acceptance is to establish an individual identity. This may include developing a balance between being single and being a parent. It is appropriate to plan for the future, but people should be aware that it is impossible to predict what they will want once they have fully processed the finality of the divorce.

6. D: Of the given pairs, sibling rivalry would likely be greatest for brothers aged 3 and 5. In general, sibling rivalry is most pronounced in same-sex siblings within three years of age. In the first eight to ten years of life, siblings tend to alternate between cooperation and competition. As they grow older, they will often spend little time together for a few years, but during adolescence will gradually develop empathy for one another. Most research suggests that adult relationships between siblings simply exaggerate the tone of the relationship of youth; that is, good relationships get better and bad relationships get worse.

7. B: Married women typically earn a lower wage than single women. This is an exception to the general trend, which is that married people are healthier, wealthier, and more content than their single counterparts. Married men are less likely to abuse alcohol and drugs, and less likely to become depressed. Married women are healthier and more likely to report satisfaction with their home lives. One reason why married women may earn less money is that they are more likely to be raising children, and therefore less focused on professional development. Despite reports about the decline of marriage, an overwhelming majority of Americans will marry at least once during their lives.

8. E: In general, accepting a stepparent is hardest for adolescent girls. Of course, this process is not easy for sons and daughters of any age. However, research suggests that the bond between a stepparent, in particular a stepfather, and an adolescent girl takes the longest to form. One possible reason for this phenomenon is that stepfathers tend to be less engaged with stepdaughters than with stepsons. The effect of remarriage on children is much the same as divorce because it involves a fundamental restructuring of the family concept. Nevertheless, stepparents who work to engage with their stepchildren can develop positive relationships over time.

9. A: Both the content and the style of family communication are important. For instance, a parent may deliver a positive message and then undermine it by demonstrating contrary behavior. The members of a family should work on communicating positively. The other answer choices are true statements about families. The decisions made by families tend to reinforce the status quo in the interest of conformity and conflict avoidance. For reasons both genetic and environmental, the members of families are likely to struggle with the same sorts of problems in life. Despite a general tendency toward stability and consistency, families inevitably change in response to the aging of each member and to pressures from the environment. Finally, it is a central tenet of family science that it is impossible to understand a family member without understanding the family as a whole.

10. D: According to John Gottman, the best response to criticism by a spouse is humor. Gottman has performed extensive research on the interactions between married couples and has identified characteristics of both durability and divorce. When the criticized partner responds to criticism by deflecting or soothing the other person, tempers are quelled and the partnership remains strong. Gottman's research suggests that there is a classic pattern of degenerating communication in an unsuccessful relationship. The pattern begins with criticism that is not directed at a certain behavior, but at the other person as a whole. In other words, the criticism of unsuccessful couples tends to lean toward character assassination. Eventually, these negative interactions lead to contempt, in which one partner openly disparages and disrespects the other. The inevitable response to contempt is defensiveness, followed by stonewalling, or a total lack of communication. When couples stop communicating, the relationship is not likely to endure.

11. B: The greatest amount of variation between people of the same age is found during early adolescence. The onset of puberty may occur at any time over the span of five years, though it typically occurs earlier in females than in males. The changes brought on by puberty are monumental and can cause rapid changes in personality, physical development, and emotional maturity. Teachers need to be aware of these changes, particularly when working with middle-school children. Family and consumer science teachers may need to act as liaisons between parents and their children, as family relationships can become strained during early adolescence.

12. A: When two children have a dispute and agree to settle it according to their mother's opinion, they are engaging in arbitration. In arbitration, two conflicting parties agree to rely on the advice of a supposedly impartial third party. Sometimes, the parties will also establish guidelines for the way a decision is to be reached. In parenting, it can be difficult to settle a dispute with arbitration, since children are unlikely to honor a decision that goes against their interests. Conciliation is a method of settling disputes in which the conflicting parties are simply asked to meet and converse, with the idea that a resolution will naturally occur as a result of this meeting. In mediation, the conflicting parties decide to enlist the aid of an impartial third party as they attempt to settle their differences. The parties in mediation do not agree to follow the advice of the third party. In negotiation, two parties try to agree on terms that are acceptable to both. Negotiation in family life is a bit like compromise. Finally, restorative justice is a system in which the person who has been wronged gets some kind of compensation from the wrongdoer. When parents force one sibling to apologize to the other, they are essentially using restorative justice.

13. C: In general, the children of working mothers have greater self-esteem. There is no one reason for this phenomenon, although one can speculate that girls might be inspired by the positive example of a successful working mother. The other answer choices are incorrect statements about working mothers. The daughters of working mothers tend to be more independent, and they are likely to have a more egalitarian view of gender relations. When the sons of working mothers are unsupervised, their performance in school tends to decline. It is very important for both parents to have a positive attitude about maternal employment, and it is especially important for husbands to support their wives in ways that can be perceived positively by children.

14. C: Structured family therapists assume that during times of conflict, family members will take sides to consolidate power. Although this process is natural, it can become problematic if the groups last for too long or create a permanent imbalance of power. A structured family therapist surveys problematic family coalitions and destabilizes them. The idea that family life is a series of actions and reactions is an assumption of Milan systemic family therapy. This approach to family therapy emphasizes patterns of behavior that lock family members into their roles, therefore inhibiting their personal growth. Behavioral family therapists assume that bad behavior persists when it is reinforced. These therapists strive to show family members how they may be inadvertently rewarding the very behavior they seek to discourage. Finally, object relations family therapists assume that ill will in a family is often a result of negative projection. In other words, the members of a family may attribute their own negative characteristics to their family members.

15. D: One drawback of inpatient treatment for alcoholism is that it is expensive. In addition, inpatient programs are often not covered by health insurance, so the patient and his or her family may be forced to pay out of pocket. The efficacy of these programs is well established, however. Some studies estimate that 70% of the participants in inpatient programs stay sober for at least five years. Many of these inpatient programs include the twelve-step process, most famously represented by Alcoholics Anonymous. Patients cannot continue to drink while they are enrolled in an inpatient program, since they are living on the grounds of the treatment facility. Finally, it is true that inpatient programs require the personal commitment of the patient, but this is true of all rehabilitation programs.

16. D: According to Piaget, the ability to imagine the mental lives of others emerges during the preoperational stage. This is the second of the four stages outlined by Piaget and typically occurs between the ages of 2 and 7. The ability to imaginatively construct the mental life of another person is called sympathy. The first stage in the Piaget model is sensorimotor, which lasts from birth until about age 2. During this time, the sense organs become activated, and the child learns about object permanence (that is, objects continue to exist even when they leave the perceptual field). In the third stage, known as concrete operational, the child improves his or her cognition and realizes that objects with different shapes may have the same volume. This stage occurs between the ages of 7 and 12. In the formal operational stage, the capacity for abstract thought is developed. When this stage occurs (and it does not occur for every person), it typically occurs after age 12. Primary socialization is not one of Piaget's stages; it is a person's first experience of living among other people. Typically, a person undergoes primary socialization within his or her family.

17. B: One example of role strain is a new teacher who struggles to maintain authority in the classroom. Role strain is any hardship a person encounters while trying to fulfill the socially accepted requirements of a role. Individuals are almost never a perfect fit for any role they attempt to inhabit, so role strain is inevitable. A public speaker who cultivates his or her expertise is displaying role performance, or the conscious fulfillment of a social role's characteristics. A person whose parents die goes through the role exit process, because he or she no longer is in the role of a son or daughter. A child who imagines what it would be like to be a police officer is demonstrating role taking, in which a person imagines what it would be like to fill a certain social role. Finally, a substitute teacher who waits tables on the weekend exemplifies the idea of the role set, or the different roles that a single person can inhabit at a given point in his or her life.

18. E: An eight year-old with the mental age of a ten year-old has an IQ (intelligence quotient) of 125. IQ is measured by dividing mental age by actual age and then multiplying the quotient. Mental age is defined as the average amount of knowledge held by a person at a given age. Of course, this is a rather arbitrary figure, dependent on the prevailing norms of education. For this reason, IQ is seen as a somewhat unreliable indicator of intellectual development. Many critics feel that it ignores intuitive, spatial, and creative abilities. The average IQ should be 100, since this is the score a person will receive when their mental age is the same as their actual age.

19. D: The student is in the contemplation stage of the transtheoretical model of change. In this stage, a person recognizes the need for a change but is not yet prepared to take action. This is the second of six stages. In the first stage, precontemplation, the person does not yet recognize that he or she has a problem. In the third stage, preparation/commitment, the

person determines that a change is necessary and begins to collect information about solutions. The fourth stage is action, when the person begins to change his or her behavior. In the fifth stage, maintenance, the person notes the benefits of the new behavior and strives to avoid falling back into bad habits. In the sixth and final stage, termination, the person has made the new behavior habitual and is very unlikely to backslide.

20. E: Echolalia is an infant's nonsensical imitation of adult speech. Most children begin exhibiting echolalia at about nine months of age. This is one of the steps in language acquisition. There are six such stages: crying, cooing, babbling, echolalia, holophrastic speech, and telegraphic speech. Over the first few months of life, an infant will develop different cries to express different emotions. After six or eight weeks, the infant will begin to display a vowel-intensive warbling sound, known as cooing. Babies between four and six months old typically begin to make a babbling noise, which over time will come to resemble the baby's native language. Echolalia is the next step, followed by holophrastic speech, in which the baby uses single words to communicate more complex ideas. Finally, between eighteen and twenty-four months, the child will initiate telegraphic speech, combinations of words that make sense together. Deep structuring is not one of the steps of language acquisition. The linguist Noam Chomsky posited that language includes a surface structure (parts of speech, vocabulary, e.g.) and a deep structure (underlying meanings of words).

21. A: The major criticism of Levinson's "seasons" of life model is that it overstates the importance of the mid-life crisis. Levinson outlined four major periods of life: infancy to adolescence; early adulthood; middle adulthood; and late adulthood. The major crisis of life according to Levinson was the realization during middle adulthood that the dreams established in early adulthood are not entirely attainable. This brings on the mid-life crisis. Subsequent psychology has indicated that this crisis does not occur for all people and is often not very severe when it does occur. However, Levinson's model does acknowledge the suffering of life and does address the last years of life, in which a person confronts and reconciles with mortality. Levinson also asserts that life transitions are made consciously and with a great deal of stress. Finally, Levinson emphasizes the role of parents in shaping the early years and thus the foundation of a person's personality development.

22. A: Sudden interest in a new hobby is not a warning sign of teen depression. Teenagers at risk of depression tend to withdraw and will not be likely to take on a new hobby. Instead, depressed teenagers lose interest in activities that previously engaged and pleased them. The other four answer choices are common warning signs of teen depression. Depression is also thought to be hereditary, so teenagers with a family history of the illness should be especially alert to these signs.

23. B: The different treatment given to students who excel in math as opposed to those who excel in English is known as horizontal socialization. Horizontal socialization is a fundamental difference in the treatment of people who inhabit different roles. Doctors and teachers, for instance, are treated differently by society, even though one profession is not necessarily prized more than the other. Vertical socialization, on the other hand, is the different treatment individuals receive when they occupy different class positions. Wealthy people, for example, are socialized differently than poor people. Resocialization is the intentional adjustment of a person's socialization, typically in the hope that the person will become better integrated into society. People who are released from prison, for instance, must be resocialized into society. Anticipatory socialization occurs when a person expects

to enter a new role in the future and adjusts his or her behavior accordingly. At the end of summer vacation, for example, students might start to adjust their clothing and hygiene as they look forward to the start of the school year. Desocialization is the relinquishing of a previously-held role. In a sense, all people are involved in a constant process of desocialization, since they are constantly casting off roles and taking on new ones.

24. D: Thrift is not one of the areas of emotional intelligence. There are five such areas: self-awareness, empathy, personal motivation, altruism, and the ability to love and be loved. These areas were outlined by the psychologist Daniel Goleman, who was one of the first experts to suggest that IQ is an insufficient measure of a person. The development of emotional intelligence is also important. It is possible to improve emotional intelligence by cultivating self-expression and learning to listen to one's conscience.

25. A: The United States actually has a higher rate of teen pregnancy than many other developed countries. However, this rate has decreased over the past twenty years, due to effective instruction and the distribution of birth control. Nevertheless, the rate of teen pregnancy remains too high, especially among Hispanics and African-Americans. Because teen pregnancy has such a damaging effect on success in life, family and consumer science teachers are encouraged to treat this subject in their discussion of family life. The Center for Disease Control offers a number of resources related to teen pregnancy.

26. A: An effective time management plan will encourage students to do the most difficult tasks first. This is considered by time management advisors to be the single most important aspect of successful time management, which is increasingly important in an age of information overload and nonstop distraction. This last point is the reason why answer choice B is incorrect: There is no way to eliminate every possible distraction. Instead, an effective time management plan should try to mitigate the damage of inevitable distractions. It is not necessary for a time management plan to be so comprehensive as to include meals, though some students may find it useful to do so. Making lists is the cornerstone of time management, since lists help students to prioritize their tasks and keep from feeling overwhelmed by the many things they have to do. Finally, because a time management plan will be tailored to the life of the individual, it will be different for each student.

27. C: When a daily routine has been established, it is less necessary to create a list of things to do. Making lists is one of the best ways to organize tasks and to keep from being overwhelmed by responsibilities. However, a daily routine makes certain tasks habitual, which can eventually eliminate the need for the list. For instance, a parent might get up every morning and go through the same steps to get his children ready for school. Since this set of tasks is performed habitually, it does not need to be written down. In addition, the development of a routine helps get the body and mind accustomed to performing certain tasks at certain times. Most people find that a routine makes it less difficult for them to find the motivation to perform unpleasant tasks.

28. D: In the system outlined by Hersey and Blanchard, the leadership style that emphasizes the performance of tasks and ignores the development of positive relationships is called telling. Hersey and Blanchard's model, known as situational leadership, describes four different leadership styles: telling, delegating, selling, and participating. These styles are distinguished by the degree to which they emphasize either task performance or

relationship building. The delegating style entails little commitment to either function. A delegating leader passes off authority to his or her subordinates. A selling leader is heavily involved with both task performance and the building of relationships. Such a leader is constantly engaged with his or her subordinates, helping them do their jobs and keeping them motivated. While a telling leader is very involved in the performance of tasks, he or she is not very interested in building positive relationships with subordinates. Such a leader is likely to micromanage subordinates, often to their annoyance. A participating leader is not involved in tasks but is very invested in his or her relationships with subordinates. Such a leader rarely asserts authority over the other members of the group.

29. D: Most of the time, the best way for a family to decide on a vacation destination is to have a discussion and then have the final decision made by the parents. It is important for parents to give their children a sense of involvement in the process, though the parents should retain the ultimate decision. When parents make decisions without consulting their children, the children are less likely to be willing to participate fully. On the other hand, when children are included in making important decisions, they often are governed by emotion or whim rather than reason. The best decision-making system, then, is a combination of discussion and parental leadership.

30. E: Of the given options, the best way to limit a child's television time is to set a timer and turn the television off when the alarm sounds. This strategy has a number of advantages. It establishes ahead of time the amount of television that can be watched, so the child will not be surprised or feel that the discipline is arbitrary. Setting up a timer also creates an objective method of enforcement with which the child cannot argue or attempt to negotiate. In this, as in many cases, it is helpful to create firm, consistent rules that the child can understand. When boundaries are consistent, the child will quickly learn the futility of arguing and will more easily come to accept the limitations on his or her desire. Scaring the child or using other negative reinforcement is a less desirable solution. Merely suggesting that the child go outside is unlikely to be influential unless it is backed up by other methods.

31. B: Group polarization is a phenomenon in which a group makes more extreme decisions than any member would make independently. Management experts believe that this is due to the desire for conformity and the subsequent reinforcement of whatever solutions are first suggested. Rather than critique another group member and create disharmony, participants will often go along and even amplify the first opinion given. Organizational conflict can actually be a healthy thing, since it indicates that views are being aired openly. Social facilitation is a phenomenon in which the presence of others encourages a person to work harder. Groupthink is similar to group polarization, except that it does not necessarily result in extreme decisions. Groupthink is the suppression of reason in the interest of maintaining group cohesion. Social loafing is a phenomenon in which people do not work as hard in a group, often because they feel their contributions will not be respected.

32. B: Members of a family are more likely to be motivated when their goal is well defined. For instance, if parents decide to save for a new car, their children will be more likely to accept material sacrifices once they know about the underlying goal of these sacrifices. People in general have a hard time accepting changes or commands when there is no communicated rationale. In addition, motivation toward a family goal tends to be higher when members volunteer their participation. A tangible reward that seems fair is another way motivation is increased. Also, the members of a family are better able to stay motivated

when they can objectively evaluate their own performance and then use this evaluation to make corrections. Finally, motivation cannot remain high when some members of the family feel that they are working much harder than other members.

33. C: Research has shown that a compressed workweek increases employee satisfaction. The normal work week consists of 5 eight-hour days; a compressed schedule increases the amount of work time for each day but decreases the number of days. Typically, the total amount of time spent at work stays the same. For instance, a common compressed workweek consists of 4 ten-hour days. There is not any demonstrated correlation between a compressed workweek and employee performance. However, employees who have a long commute are generally very enthusiastic about such a plan, since it eliminates one commute to and from the office. This advantage would be irrelevant to employees who work from home.

34. A: The first step towards eliminating wasted time is to keep a log of how time is spent. In the chaotic modern world, almost everyone feels as if he or she is moving in a dozen different directions at once. The natural result is the creeping suspicion that time is being wasted and maximum productivity is not being achieved. Time management experts agree that the first step in eliminating wasted time is to determine where it is being wasted. This is done by keeping an activity log for several days and then studying it to find where time is typically wasted. Once the time wasters have been identified, it will become easier to tighten up the daily schedule.

35. D: A five year-old is probably too young to mop the kitchen floor. Mopping requires a degree of upper-body strength that a child of this age is unlikely to possess. However, a five year-old should be able to complete all of the other tasks listed as answer choices. Moreover, children at this age are often very enthusiastic about helping with household chores, particularly if they are given a chance to work independently. At this age, children are interested in participating in adult activities whenever possible, and parents should take advantage of this interest.

36. A: The proper decision-making process begins by defining the problem to be solved. Too often, students start working on potential solutions before the problem has been fully articulated. This leads to half-measures and ineffective decisions. Only after the problem has been outlined in its entirety should possible solutions be considered. It is a good idea to write down these options. Whenever possible, the emphasis should be on long-term solutions rather than quick fixes. In some cases, it may be determined that there is not enough information to make an informed decision. If this is the case, either information should be collected or, if this is impossible, the decision maker should figure out a strategy for mitigating this problem.

37. D: When making a schedule, children should be encouraged to both include some free time and place the hardest tasks first. However, children should not be encouraged to block out long stretches for completing all homework because this would be too vague. One of the hallmarks of an effective schedule is specificity, so large categories like homework should be broken down into smaller tasks. At the least, the child should divide homework into subjects, and it may even be necessary to subdivide subjects into particular tasks. It is important, however, for a schedule to include some free time because interruptions and distractions are inevitable. If a schedule is too rigid, the student is likely to become

discouraged when he or she is unable to meet it. Also, it is a good idea to place the hardest tasks first, since the student will have the highest energy and mental resources then.

38. B: Drop-in child care is useful when the regular childcare provider is unavailable. Drop-in child care is a service offered by some daycares and other child care centers. When parents have a specific need for childcare, when their normal provider is closed, for instance, they can call the drop-in center and see if there is any room for their child. The parents will need to have registered with the drop-in center ahead of time. This arrangement helps child care facilities operate at maximum capacity and helps parents fill unexpected holes in their child care schedule. Drop-in child care can be expensive, however, and may not be a valid option for children with special needs. Whether a child is in school or not would have little bearing on the utility of drop-in child care.

39. D: One disadvantage of dealing with consumer finance companies is that they often charge high interest rates. Consumer finance companies lend money to private citizens who want to make a purchase. There are few lending restrictions related to the purpose of the loan. Because these loans are considered to be risky, consumer finance companies often charge exorbitant interest rates. In most cases, however, they will accept property as security. The high interest rates and predatory business practices associated with consumer finance companies should dissuade consumers from dealing with them unless absolutely necessary. Before entering into an agreement with a consumer finance company, one should consider whether the planned purchase is absolutely necessary.

40. E: Restaurants are the most common employer of high-school students. This assertion is based on data from the United States Bureau of Labor Statistics. The presence of so many students in food service jobs can be useful to both the family and the consumer science teacher. These students will have direct experience with the cost of food, as well as with the nutritional choices available in a restaurant. It is an excellent idea to allow students to incorporate their work experience into classroom activities.

41. A: Borrowers with a poor credit rating will not be eligible for a bank's prime rate. The prime rate is the lowest rate of interest offered by a commercial bank or other lending institution. It is made available only to borrowers with pristine credit ratings, since these people and businesses are most likely to repay the loan according to the agreed-upon schedule. Savings deposits, demand deposits, and certificates of deposit are all investitures made by the consumer in a bank, and therefore do not depend on credit rating. A savings deposit can be withdrawn at any time, while a certificate of deposit must be kept in the bank for a prescribed length of time. A demand deposit is essentially the same thing as a checking account, because the funds within it can be withdrawn at any time and in any amount. Banks are required to have deposit insurance to guarantee that they will be able to return the funds invested by customers.

42. E: Research suggests that children in daycare are better at articulating their desires. It is believed that this ability develops because the child is dealing with a caregiver who, unlike the child's parent, may not intuit demands. The other answer choices are false statements. Research shows that children in daycare are more likely to be aggressive and disobedient, perhaps because they feel the need to advocate their own interests away from home. Doctors emphasize the importance of establishing the parent-child bond before starting daycare. Children in daycare make friends more easily, perhaps because they get more

practice at interacting with others. The value of daycare is closely correlated with the quality of the supervision.

43. B: Presidents Kennedy and Nixon did not include the right to affordability among the consumer rights asserted during the 1960s. Businesses do not have any obligation to sell products at prices within reach of the average consumer. There were five essential consumer rights promulgated at that time: the right to a safe product; the right to redress; the right to be heard; the right to be informed; and the right to choose. The government enforces laws that require businesses to sell safe products or to clearly warn consumers about products that are not always safe. The right to redress enables consumers to receive a refund or compensation of some kind when a product does them harm. Consumers have a right to speak and be acknowledged by businesses. Consumers also have a right to as much information about products as they desire. Finally, consumers have a right to choose among a variety of products; it is with this in mind that the government enforces laws against monopoly.

44. D: It is generally agreed that a family should spend no more than 25% of its income on housing. Although some lenders are willing to give money to homebuyers who will spend up to 40% of their income on housing, this is considered a risky loan. Such a loan is especially risky when the borrower has other long-term debt besides housing costs. As a consumer, it is wise to create a detailed budget before committing any funds to housing costs.

45. C: Purchasing a DVD is a discretionary expense because it is based on personal desire rather than need. In other words, it is an expense made at the discretion of the consumer. Discretionary expenses are those over which a consumer has the most control. A comprehensive budget must include discretionary expenses as well as fixed and variable expenses. Fixed expenses, such as rent, are the same every month. Variable expenses, including groceries, school supplies, and heating oil, are always present but vary in amount over the course of a year.

46. C: For most people, it makes sense to set up a personal budget on a monthly basis. Expenses such as rent and bills tend to be due on a monthly basis, and a month is long enough that brief fluctuations in food costs will balance out. Of course, a person needs to be sensitive to the fact that some months will be more expensive than others. For instance, if a person lives in a cold climate, he or she is likely to spend more money on heating during the winter months. Those who get paid every week or every two weeks will need to make a simple calculation to determine their monthly earnings.

47. B: If Denise has a credit card with an APR of 4.5% and she maintains an average balance of $2500 throughout the year, the account will accrue $112.50 in interest. APR stands for annual percentage rate; it is the amount of interest charged over the course of twelve months. To calculate the amount of interest accruing on Denise's account, multiply her average balance by the APR (making sure to convert 4.5% into the decimal 0.045). The product of this calculation is the amount of interest accrued on the account over the course of a year.

48. D: It is not a good idea to visit fewer than three daycare providers before selecting one. Each of these visits should be thorough and should include a full tour and an extensive conversation with the care providers. Beforehand, a parent or guardian should make a list of questions for the meeting. For instance, one should get a description of a typical day at the facility, as well as spend some time observing the childcare providers at work. Whenever possible, children should visit the daycare facility before starting to go there regularly. Toilet training is handled differently by different provides, so if this is an issue, parents should inquire about the institutional policy. Children should be allowed to bring a favorite toy, blanket, or stuffed animal to daycare. Parents or guardians, especially those for whom this is the first daycare experience, should visit at least three daycare facilities before making a decision. Finally, parents or guardians should try to discuss going to daycare with their child in a positive manner as early as possible.

49. E: A debenture bond is secured only by the assets and earnings of the corporation that issues it. This is just one kind of bond sold by corporations to raise money. Consumers should be apprised of the various types of bonds offered so that they can make wise investment decisions. The general difference between bonds is the security offered; that is, the way in which the corporation guarantees repayment. A collateral trust bond uses the stocks and bonds of other companies as collateral. A mortgage bond is secured by a piece of mortgaged property, such as an office building or factory. A sinking-fund bond is a form of debenture bond in which the corporation additionally pledges to pay back the money slowly over a long time. A convertible bond can be traded in for common stock at any time.

50. D: The major benefit of vitamin A is that it helps the body produce healthy hair and skin. Carrots, pumpkins, fish, and eggs are all good sources of vitamin A. Help with forming new cells is a major benefit of folate, or folic acid. There is a great deal of folate in spinach and fortified grains. Vitamin C is one of the primary disease-fighting nutrients. It is obtained most effectively from citrus fruits and broccoli. Concentration and alertness are improved by vitamin B-12. It is most abundant in fish, poultry, and eggs. Calcium is a mineral that helps muscles contract. It is abundant in dairy products and sardines.

51. A: The United States Department of Agriculture recommends between six and eleven servings of bread, cereal, rice, and pasta daily. This is the most recommended servings of all the food groups. The other recommended serving amounts are as follows: vegetables (three to five servings); fruits (two to four servings); milk, yogurt, and cheese (two to three servings); meat, poultry, fish, eggs, dry beans, and nuts (two to three servings); and fats, oils, and sweets (less than a serving).

52. C: The recommended daily values listed on food packaging assume a daily diet of two thousand calories. Adult males are generally advised to eat about this many calories every day. Women and children, however, may require fewer calories, while athletes may require more. When one's recommended caloric intake is considerably lower or higher than two thousand, one must make necessary adjustments to the daily values.

53. B: Food manufacturers now add folic acid to their products because it has been shown to reduce the risk of spinal bifida in infants. Folic acid is a B vitamin that aids in the synthesis of hemoglobin, which is required to transport oxygen throughout the bloodstream. Pregnant women, women who are trying to become pregnant, and elderly

people should all ensure that their diet includes foods with folic acid. There are also a number of safe supplements containing folic acid.

54. A: Losing weight quickly decreases the metabolism. Nutritionists and doctors believe that this is a form of self-defense by the body, which senses that food is not as available and therefore tries to limit its use of calories. All of the other answer choices are events that increase metabolism. Weight gain always raises metabolism, in part because there is more muscle or fat to provide with nutrients. Muscle burns more calories than fat, so an increase in muscle mass will correlate with an increase in metabolism. Any exercise tends to increase metabolism.

55. D: An ovo-lacto-vegetarian is a person who eats fruits, vegetables, grains, dairy products, and eggs. These people get most of their proteins from beans, eggs, milk, and cheese. There are several other kinds of vegetarians. A vegan is someone who eats only plant foods; vegans do not eat any meat or animal product, including honey. Lacto-vegetarians eat fruits, vegetables, grains, and dairy products.

56. A: A person should consume 100 milligrams of major minerals, including sodium and chloride, every day. Of course, sodium and chloride can both be obtained from table salt. Some of the other major minerals are potassium, calcium, phosphorus, and magnesium. Trace minerals, such as iron, zinc, and copper, need only be consumed at a rate of 10 milligrams every day. The precise effect of these minerals on the body has not yet been determined.

57. E: Vitamin C is water-soluble, meaning that it is absorbed into the blood stream and can be forced out of the body through urine and sweat. For example, caffeinated beverages can increase the urine stream and thereby diminish the absorption of water-soluble nutrients like vitamin C. Vitamin B is another water-soluble nutrient. Other vitamins, including A, D, E, and K, are absorbed by the intestinal membrane; these vitamins are said to be fat-soluble. Vitamin D can also be obtained from sunlight.

58. C: An overconsumption of protein can put strain on the kidneys and liver. This is one reason why doctors discourage the use of body-building supplements and protein shakes unless under medical supervision. An excessive consumption of protein can lead to general imbalances in diet, which can undermine fitness in the long run. Protein does contribute to the development of muscle mass, but this is not necessarily a problem. Weight-lifting and vigorous physical activities require complex carbohydrates as well as proteins.

59. D: Palm oil is not an unsaturated fat. On the contrary, it is a saturated fat, meaning that excessive consumption of it can lead to heart disease. Coconut oil, butter, and lard are some of the other saturated fats. The other answer choices are unsaturated fats, which are better for the body. In fact, olive oil and canola oil can reduce the amount of cholesterol in the body.

60. B: A calorie is the amount of energy required to raise the temperature of one gram of water by one degree Celsius. In the United States, every packaged food must contain a listing of the number of calories per serving. Also, whereas in the past it was possible for manufacturers to confuse the consumer by indicating odd serving sizes, the designation of

serving size is now regulated by the federal government. All the manufacturers of a particular product are required to use similar serving sizes.

61. D: A person who is 41 to 100% heavier than his or her ideal weight is moderately obese. Health professionals have divided obesity into three degrees: mild, moderate, and severe. A person who is less than 20% heavier than his or her ideal weight is considered merely overweight, but a person who is 20 to 40% heavier is considered mildly obese. People who are more than 100% heavier than their ideal weight are severely obese. Moderately obese people are much more likely to have diabetes or osteoporosis, but do not necessarily suffer from these conditions.

62. E: All three of the statements are true. Bulimia can lead to tooth decay, due to a combination of malnutrition and corrosion by stomach acid. Anorexics often have a distorted self-image, believing themselves to be much heavier than they actually are. Finally, bulimia does not always include purging (induced vomiting or defecation). Bulimics may obsessively exercise or abstain from food in order to lose weight. Both anorexia and bulimia are extremely dangerous and should be discussed at great length in the nutrition component of a family and consumer science class. These conditions are especially common among middle-school and high-school students.

63. B: Dairy products do not contain significant amounts of iron. The other answer choices, however, are nutrients that are abundant in dairy products. Riboflavin is another nutrient found in great quantities in dairy products. According to the USDA, people should eat two or three servings of dairy every day. A serving is equivalent to eight ounces of milk, a cup of yogurt, or one and a half ounces of cheese. People should be careful about which dairy products they consume, as many contain a great deal of fat.

64. B: Vitamin D is known to help the body absorb the phosphorus and calcium obtained through a person's diet. It is present in small amounts in foods like fish and eggs and is especially present in cod liver oil. Vitamin E is a major antioxidant, meaning that it eliminates cells that can have a deleterious effect on the body. This vitamin is found in good amounts in wheat germ oil, milk, and plant leaves. Vitamin B-3, also known as niacin, helps to reduce levels of cholesterol in the blood. It is found in yeast, dairy products, and wheat germ. Vitamin K promotes blood clotting. It is abundant in spinach, cabbage, and soybeans. Vitamin A contributes to the growth and maintenance of body tissues. It is particularly present in eggs, spinach, and liver.

65. E: Stained clothing should be cleaned within 24 hours; after a day, many stains will have set and will be almost impossible to remove. The other answer choices are false statements about stain removal. It is not a good idea to iron stained objects, as the heat is likely to set the stain. Bar soap should not be used on fresh stains, because it too has the capacity to set stains. Hot water can set stains caused by proteins, like blood, milk, and egg. It is not considered safe to wash clothing with chemical stains alongside regular laundry. Although most washing machines are strong enough to remove toxic chemicals, there is no sense in taking the risk.

66. C: Quilting is the fabrication method of stitching a liner fabric in between two outer fabrics. Because this process essentially creates a three-layered fabric, it is used in outerwear and clothing that is meant for cold weather. Knitting is the use of hooked needles

to loop yarn threads together. Fabrics made by knitting tend to be very flexible. In stitch-through, a web of fiber is stitched together by a chain of smaller stitches. This technique is also known as malimo. Tufting is a process in which a woven backing has yarns inserted into it, where they are sealed in place with glue. This process, commonly used in the manufacture of carpets, is occasionally used in apparel as well. Finally, weaving is the creation of a network of three yarns, interconnected at right angles throughout the fabric.

67. A: Wool that has been combed into parallel threads and then spun into a fine yarn is known as worsted. Renowned for its strength, worsted is used in dresses and suits. Cashmere is an especially soft form of wool that is created from the hair of a specific Indian goat. Angora is another high-end wool made from the long hairs of the angora rabbit. Polyester is a synthetic textile, meaning that it is not made from plants or animals. It is often blended with other fibers in the creation of clothing. Spandex is a synthetic textile with amazing flexibility.

68. D: When the fuzzy fibers of a fabric ball up and adhere to the outside of the garment, they are said to be pilling. The degree to which a fabric "pills" is one criteria of durability. Fuzzing is the emergence of tiny fibers from a yarn, creating the effect of roughness on the outside of the garment. Snagging occurs when fibers catch and are pulled out of the weave. Breathing is the ability of a loosely woven fabric to allow the passage of air. Light fabrics tend to be better at breathing. Creasing is the creation of permanent folds in the fabric. Oftentimes, pants will be worn with an intentional crease along the front and back of the legs.

69. B: When it appears on a clothing label, the word *carded* means that the garment was made from short, thick cotton fibers. The use of carded fibers creates a fabric that is soft and strong. When the garment is made of long, straight cotton fibers, it is said to be combed. A combed fabric is smoother and shinier. A garment that only contains one type of fiber is considered pure. Garments that have been subjected to a permanent or durable press are more resistant to wrinkles. These processes are usually noted on the clothing label. A label may also indicate whether a garment has been inspected and that it was not created in a sweat shop.

70. E: Of the given garments, a pair of wool pants would be the most resistant to wrinkles. Because of the thickness of the fiber and the general looseness of the weave, clothing made of wool tends to be very resistant to wrinkles. This is one reason why wool clothing is so useful for travel; it can be packed in a suitcase and not need to be ironed later. Silk and cotton products are moderately resistant to wrinkles. If packed properly, they can be worn without needing to be ironed. Rayon and linen are notoriously prone to wrinkles. Clothing made of these materials must be washed, dried, and stored properly.

71. A: One common problem with silk clothing is that it is easily damaged by the sun. Silken garments can fade quickly if they are not kept out of direct sunlight. For this reason, silk should be kept in a drawer or dark closet. The other answer choices are false statements. Silk is very resistant to abrasions and wrinkles, and it burns very slowly. Silk is renowned for its smoothness. It is considered one of the least coarse fabrics in the world.

72. B: The FTC does not mandate that clothing labels indicate whether the garment contains mink or rabbit. These fibers are considered to be specialty wools; therefore, they do not need to be identified by anything other than the word "wool" on the label. Fur labels, on the other hand, must declare the animal species and country of origin on the label. All of the other answer choices are pieces of information that must be included on a label. The label must name any fiber that represents more than 5% of the product's weight. The country in which the garment was processed and manufactured must be indicated. Only when clothing is made in the United States and entirely from American materials can it be designated as "Made in the USA."

73. C: It is safe to use bleach on cotton if it is done so occasionally. If bleach is frequently applied to cotton or other cellulosic fibers, the fabric may be damaged. Bleach should not be used on any other fabrics, as it has the ability to cause serious damage. Bleach will often dissolve fabrics made of hair fibers, such as silk, wool, and cashmere. Although bleach can be a valuable tool for fabric cleaning, it must be used sparingly to avoid irreversible damage to fibers.

74. D: Of the given fabrics, black satin would offer the best protection against sunlight. Dark clothing tends to protect the body from ultraviolet radiation better, because they absorb rather than reflect the rays of the sun. Moreover, densely woven fabrics like satin have fewer holes through which sunlight can flow. Of course, black satin might not be the most comfortable fabric to wear in the sun. Dark clothing gets very hot, and sweating in satin clothing can be unpleasant. Many people prefer to wear cotton clothing, because the looser weave allows for superior ventilation. However, cotton offers little protection against UV rays, so it is important to wear sunscreen under the clothing.

75. E: In interior design, the arrangement of elements in a pattern around some central point is known as radial balance. For instance, a dining room might be arranged such that all of the furniture extends out from a central table. The pattern of the radial elements can be based on size, color, or texture. Symmetrical balance is the arrangement of identical elements around a center point or line. This is the most rigidly balanced form of interior design. Gradation balance is the subtle but regular alteration of specific elements in an interior. For instance, a room might include various shades of the same color. Asymmetrical balance is the arrangement of unlike elements that nevertheless creates a balance when looked at as a whole. Harmonic balance is the agreement of the various design elements in a room. It does not entail any particular physical arrangement.

76. B: In a dumbbell layout pattern, spaces are arranged along a linear path, with major elements at either end. This layout pattern is appropriate for houses or buildings in which there are two main places of activity, and it is a good idea to keep the areas separate. A radial layout consists of a number of paths extending out from a central point. This kind of arrangement is typical of offices and buildings with one central purpose. In a clustered layout, several spaces with similar size, shape, and function are grouped close together and linked along a central space or corridor. A doughnut layout, as exemplified by the Pentagon, consists of a circular corridor with rooms on either side. A centralized layout consists of secondary elements arranged around a central point, or axis. One example of a centralized layout is a plaza, in which the central point may be a statue or fountain.

77. A: The Fibonacci sequence, in which each successive number is the sum of the two previous numbers, begins 0, 1, 1, 2, 3, 5. The Fibonacci sequence is one of the classic proportions used frequently in interior design. It occurs often in nature and has been found to be pleasing to the eye. The quantities of the Fibonacci sequence may be numbers of units or distances.

78. C: Housing experts consider air temperature to be the most important determinant of human comfort. There are a number of factors that influence human comfort, but the primary concern for most people with regard to housing is to be kept warm and dry. In general, a house needs to be between 69 and 80 degrees Fahrenheit in order for its inhabitants to be comfortable. The other answer choices are other factors that affect comfort. Relative humidity is the moisture content of the air relative to the amount of moisture that could be in the air at that temperature without condensing. People tend to be comfortable in houses that maintain a relative humidity from 30 to 65%. Mean radiant temperature is the degree to which a person's temperature changes because of radiation. Depending on the air temperature and ventilation of a room, the people and objects within it will either absorb or give off heat. It is more comfortable to absorb heat than to lose it. Air quality is the amount of pollutants and noxious vapors in the atmosphere. Obviously, air quality correlates to comfort. Ventilation is the degree to which the air in a room circulates freely. The amount of ventilation appropriate for a room will depend on its intended use. Kitchens and bathrooms, for instance, tend to benefit from more ventilation.

79. A: Curtains are fabric hung across the window by a rod and cover either the extreme ends of the window or the entire window. The major difference between curtains and draperies is that curtains are hung from a rod and typically lay closer to the window. A louvered shutter is a hard panel in front of a window. The panel consists of one or more planes that can be opened and closed. A grille is a permanent window covering, usually made of metal. Grilles are generally aimed at reducing the amount of light that flows in through a window. A Roman shade is a translucent, accordion-like panel that is raised or lowered with a cord.

80. D: The gross area of the kitchen is 156 square feet. In interior design, the gross area of a room is its area, as well as the areas of any ancillary spaces. Pantries, closets, and similar spaces are considered ancillary. The area of a room is found by multiplying length by width. Sometimes, the length of a pantry or closet will be referred to as depth. If the shape of a space is irregular (for instance, L-shaped), it is best to divide the room into rectangular spaces, find the areas of these spaces, and then add them together.

81. E: Polyester is the synthetic woodwork finish that creates a durable surface. It is an opaque finish, meaning that it obscures the natural look of the lumber underneath. Lacquer, polyurethane, and varnish are the other three popular opaque woodwork finishes. Polyurethane is quite durable as well, but it can be difficult to repair when it is damaged. Varnish can be either opaque or transparent; it is usually easier to apply than lacquer. Vinyl is a transparent finish that is resistant to degradation by moisture and chemicals.

82. B: It is not a good idea to encourage learning-disabled students to strive for perfection. Of course, perfection is an admirable goal, but students with learning disabilities will likely have struggled at times in school and may become discouraged if they fail to reach an impossible standard. Instead, teachers should give students positive reinforcement

whenever they make progress. The other answer choices are sound strategies for working with learning-disabled students. Such students can be overwhelmed by complex tasks, even when they are capable of accomplishing each of the constituent steps. Students with learning disabilities thrive when they are given a specific routine for the school day. Such students often become confused and unruly when they do not know what they are supposed to be doing. Students with attention deficit disorder may benefit from lessons that incorporate motion and tactile learning. Because such students often have a surplus of nervous energy, they are better able to focus when they are physically occupied. Finally, dialogue is a great way to introduce abstract concepts to students with learning disabilities. Often, these students need more opportunity to ask questions and receive clarification of difficult concepts.

83. E: The ability to create a personal budget is one of the cognitive objectives of consumer science. Cognitive objectives emphasize intellectual skills, including analysis, synthesis, and evaluation. The creation of a budget requires a student to assemble all information related to income and expenses and to organize that information in a comprehensible table. The abilities to select drapes and restrain consumer impulses are affective objectives, since they require the student to manage his or her emotions and consult his or her taste. The ability to arrange furniture is arguably an affective and psychomotor objective, since it requires physical activity as well as aesthetic sense. The ability to load a shopping cart is a purely psychomotor objective.

84. A: One common criticism of cooperative education programs is that they isolate students from the rest of the academic community. In a cooperative education program, students actually participate in some of the businesses and organizations they are learning about in consumer education class. These programs provide direct on-the-job training and help students make informed career choices later in life. These programs also increase contact between the business and academic communities, which can be rejuvenating for both sectors. Finally, research suggests that cooperative education programs actually increase student motivation, perhaps because they show students the direct application of what they are learning in school.

85. C: Community service is not a focus on Junior Achievement programs at the high school-level. This is not to say that JA programs are indifferent to business ethics. However, the emphasis of Junior Achievement is to prepare students for success in the business community after their education is complete. To this end, the programs administered by JA focus on economics, personal finance, work preparation, and business and entrepreneurship. Junior Achievement is a non-profit organization that is active in most schools due to the support of corporate and private donations.

86. C: The primary focus of Family, Career, and Community Leaders is the family. Indeed, this is the only in-school student organization that focuses primarily on the family. Since 1945, this organization has worked in all grades to promote the understanding of family roles and responsibilities and to encourage communication between family members and the community at large. Some of the particular points of emphasis for the FCCLA are personal responsibility, community service, and family education.

87. A: A needs assessment for a family and consumer science program should begin with a gap analysis, in which the performance of the class is compared to the performance of students at leading schools. While this may involve a survey of summative assessment results, it should also include a look at the instructional methods, equipment, and community support at the respective schools. This process is similar to the benchmarking performed by business leaders, wherein a business is compared to its most successful competitor. The idea is to bring one's own performance in line with the top performer in one's field. The subsequent needs analysis will define the ways in which the family and consumer science program should improve its approach to leaders in the field.

88. C: A list of community resources is not one of the necessary components of an effective syllabus. A syllabus is essential for organizing the structure and content of a family and consumer science class. Many students do not know what such a course entails, so the syllabus should include a clear mission statement and outline of the course content. The mission statement should state the specific goals of the class. The syllabus should also include clear assessment objectives and an explanation of the grading scale to be used. Experienced teachers know that making the assessment and grading protocols explicit at the beginning of the year can eliminate a great deal of trouble later on.

89. A: Dyssemia is a learning disability that might prevent a student from succeeding in a role-play activity. Dyssemia is a disorder which makes it hard to distinguish social cues and signals. A student with this problem would have a difficult time interpreting the gestures and underlying emotions of his or her fellow participants. Dyssemic students require special instruction about reading another person's body language and vocal tone. Apraxia is a learning disability that inhibits the ability to coordinate movements to accomplish a particular goal. Dysgraphia is associated with difficulty in writing and spelling. Dyslexia is a broad category of language-related learning disabilities that extend beyond reading. Visual perception disorders make it hard for students to identify written words and symbols.

90. E: Of the given factors, an affiliation with the United States government is the least important consideration in the evaluation of Internet research. There are a number of federal government websites that can be valuable for a family and consumer science teacher, but this affiliation is not a guarantee of utility. The Internet can be a great resource for information about family and consumer science, but an educator must ensure that the information obtained online is accurate and from a reputable source. The other four answer choices are factors that should receive consideration when a person is deciding whether a website is credible. Trustworthy websites, especially those connected with universities and government departments, have an editorial board that approves content. The organization that maintains the website should be easy to discover and investigate. A good website is likely to have links to other, similar websites. Just as we can tell a lot about people by their friends, so we can tell a lot about a site by its links. A trustworthy website will be updated frequently.

91. E: A number of high-school students believe that the most important content area in family and consumer science is food and nutrition. Moreover, this is the most popular family and consumer science subject among high-school students. Perhaps this is because food and nutrition are more relevant to the current lives of high-school students, especially those who are concerned with their physical appearance and health. Housing, family development, and personal finance may not yet be pertinent subjects in the lives of young

people. It is incumbent upon the family and consumer sciences teacher, then, to emphasize the importance of these subjects.

92. A: The original purpose of family and consumer science education was to redress social problems such as child labor and the repression of women. In the last years of the nineteenth century, Ellen Swallow Richards convened a group of social reform-minded educators at Lake Placid, New York, to develop programs for domestic economy and household management. These programs were the beginning of what has become family and consumer science education. It is important for teachers to acknowledge that the roots of this subject are in social reform. Even now, the underlying intention of family and consumer science education should be to empower students in their family lives by teaching them to manage their finances and consumer decisions.

93. D: Setting up a mock storefront for a retail business is one way to develop the psychomotor skills of elementary-school students. Psychomotor skills are best acquired through physical action. Setting up a storefront is one such activity, since the best way to learn about product placement is to practice it rather than read or be told about it. Learning to calculate compound interest and looking up banking terms in the dictionary are activities that develop cognitive skills. Drawing a picture of one's ideal house is a good way to develop affective skills. The creation of a budget for a school wardrobe requires a combination of cognitive and affective skills, insofar as the students will need to decide which clothes they want to buy and then work out a comprehensive pricing list.

94. B: One advantage of large classes is that they tend to have greater access to resources. Large classes have more students, and therefore more connections to the community. These connections can be extremely useful in a family and consumer science class. Also, schools are likely to apportion more equipment and financial resources to larger classes. For these reasons, teachers of large classes often have excellent resources at their disposal. The other answer choices are false statements. Large classes tend to create poorer relations between students and teacher, as there are simply too many students for the teacher to establish close relations with each one. Large classes tend to limit the teaching methods that can be used, since some activities are not manageable with a large group. Teachers must keep records for every student, so it stands to reason that larger classes will create more paperwork. Finally, most teachers are more comfortable in an intimate setting with just a few students.

95. A: Experience is not considered a relevant factor when making changes in the family and consumer sciences curriculum. Teachers of all levels of experience should be able to adapt their method and content when called upon to do so. In recent years, there has been pressure for the family and consumer science curriculum to be more closely aligned with general content standards. Teachers do report that knowledge, time, skill, and expense can be significant barriers to change in the curriculum. In particular, many teachers claim that they do not have enough time to implement major changes. The knowledge and skill obstacles may not be the fault of the teacher; for instance, a teacher might not get approval for changes from an administrator who is ignorant about the subject.

96. E: When dividing students up into groups for a project, the best way to avoid gender discrimination is to assign leadership positions to boys and girls in each group. Answer choice D is also a good idea, but it is implicit in answer choice E. Groups should never be

segregated by gender unless there is a specific reason for doing so. Also, students should be discouraged from always performing the tasks stereotypically associated with their gender. For example, boys should be encouraged to assume roles related to the arts, while girls should be given opportunities to work with math and science. For most teachers, the best defense against gender discrimination is awareness and a commitment to equal treatment for all students.

97. C: The primary determinant of whether a teacher will adopt instructional technology is perceived usefulness. The cost of the technology is basically irrelevant to the teacher, since it is the school or district that will bear the cost. Student interest is of some importance, since the technology will not be successful unless it is engaging to the students. However, there are plenty of engaging technologies that have little application in the classroom. Geographic location has very little bearing on adoption of technology, since most equipment is available in all parts of the country. Finally, the teacher's aptitude is slightly less important than perceived usefulness, since most teachers assume that they can learn how to use new technologies in a fairly short time.

98. B: The Carl D. Perkins Improvement Act of 2006 mandated that the curriculum of family and consumer science be aligned with general content standards. This act is an offshoot of the No Child Left Behind Act. Its intention is to boost proficiency by ensuring that the content of family and consumer science classes reinforces general academic knowledge. It is part of a general effort to standardize career and technical (formerly known as vocational) education.

99. D: An activity that requires students to describe their ideal home falls within the affective domain. This domain of education encompasses all of the emotional responses to subjects. A child's emotional responses evolve in a manner similar to their intellectual and physical responses. When students are asked to describe his or her ideal house, they are essentially organizing imaginative elements into a coherent response. This management of the imagination is an important skill. The affective domain is one of three outlined in Bloom's taxonomy. The other two are the psychomotor and cognitive domains, concerned with physical and intellectual skills, respectively.

100. E: Between the ages of six and eight, children should develop the ability to count coins. In the first few years of school, children should learn the values of the various coins, and should be able to assemble different combinations of coins to produce the same value. At this age, children should understand the general purpose of a bank and a savings account. Some children at this age will be able to manage a small allowance. All of the other answer choices are more advanced skills. Making change, comparing prices, maintaining records, and using banking terms are skills not typically developed until at least age nine.